modern
psychoanalysis

Contents

ii

The Phyllis W. Meadow award for excellence in psychoanalytic writing

The editors

This year's award-winning essays bring a variety of theoretical and philosophical perspectives to bear on our profession's applications in the treatment room and to the culture that serves as the matrix in which our therapeutic work proceeds. Jonathan Dunn's article comparing some of Freud's ideas with those of Hans Loewald is the first serious consideration this journal has given to that important and interesting psychoanalytic thinker and philosopher of mind. Marilyn Charles's essay is centrally concerned with connecting the clinical process of psychoanalysis with the impact of the surrounding culture on the character of a particular patient. Her thinking is influenced by Lacan, who is by no means new to modern psychoanalysts or to these pages. David Greven adds a literary-critical perspective to his psychoanalytic readings in a penetrating and profoundly respectful critique of Freud's writings on narcissism, particularly in relation to male homosexuality. Josie Oppenheim has noticed that intimations of magic can be a crucial component of the identity of adoptive children, to themselves and those around them. In focusing on the preoedipal ground of that phenomenon, her thoughts on the subject are particularly modern analytic.

The foundational wisdom in Freud's and Loewald's metapsychologies*

Jonathan Dunn

The author maintains that both Freud and Loewald conceive mental life dialectically, as the interaction between mutually defining, interdependent polar sides of psychological experience. The major dialectical tension addressed is mind as a closed vs. mind as an open system, metapsychologically seen in Freud's instinct theories and Loewald's revisions. Wisdom is related to how both theorists strive to stay open to and integrate the mind's dialectical nature.

The thin line between wisdom and foolishness makes this discussion risky. Like all opposite human experiences, they are peculiary enmeshed. How easily, for instance, just a hairline too much assertion of wisdom can flip into humiliation, or how intertwined the word *sapient*, which means extremely wise and discerning, seems to be with the words *sap* and *sappy*, which imply gullibility and silliness. Indeed, I am not always sure if my ideas about wisdom are on target or off the mark (wise or silly). But this is to be expected, given the ambiguous, paradoxical nature of mental life. From this perspective, my struggle to balance both feelings exemplifies a personal "living out" of my major thesis on wisdom, which I will explain as I go. I am reminded of something Jonathan Lear (2003) wrote that bears heavily on the method I've used in this paper:

> Psychoanalysis is a subjective category: the process of shaping oneself into a psychoanalyst is one that never comes to an end.

*The following colleagues helped me think through and organize this paper: Jim Dimon, Michael Wagner, Bram Fridhandler, Mitchel Wilson, Lee Grossman, Wendy Stern, and Steven Goldberg.

The process of actively and understandingly living with one's conflicts . . . is itself the life of becoming a certain kind of subject. It
is not something one completes once and for all; it is something
that is always fresh, always beginning. It is only when one gets
trapped by one's conflicts that things get old, that one starts to go
dead as a subject. (pp. 91, 96–97)

This passage opened my mind; to me, it seemed a wise approach
to psychoanalysis, albeit a deceptively difficult one. It contextu-
alizes psychoanalysis not as an external entity that one tries to
conform to, but as an ever-evolving, internally mandated creation through which each analyst must express herself and live.
Personalizing analysis in this way requires and, in turn, propels
a generative open-mindedness that keys effective analytic understanding and clinical process. I try to stay true to this understanding. But by so doing I try to do more. I want to explore, in
our theory-making, clinical activity, and analytic process, how
we maintain the receptiveness to ourselves and to our patients
that such open-mindedness entails.

My ultimate goal is to illuminate the wisdom rooted in Lear's
invitation and challenge. To this end, I don't focus squarely on
the analyst's curiosity, nor do I mention specific analytic behaviors or techniques. Rather, I am reaching for an intellectual
sensibility and form, an underlying emotional tone that reflects
a foundational wisdom through which these and other such elements of analytic work are communicated. I see the bearings
of this foundation emanating from Freud's metapsychology
and Loewald's revisions. My discussion also leans on Schafer's
(1976, chapt. 3; 1983) conception of an analytic attitude and
vision of reality, which he describes in the clinical setting as
something "implied—between the lines—in the analytic mode
of understanding" (1976, p. 46). The analyst's influence in this
context is indirect. It permeates the clinical environment and
is absorbed by the analysand, mostly unconsciously. This type
of communication depends not so much on the words that are
spoken, as important as they may be, but instead on how, when,
and in what emotional context they are uttered.

A major premise of my discussion is that indirect transmission
of the analyst's wisdom hinges on her capacity to think dialectically. By this I mean an ability to interpretively grasp the manner
in which dichotomous aspects of psychic experience and motiva-

tion, through balance and synthesis, transform the nature (and our comprehension) of the other. The psyche is captured by this form of thinking as an amalgamation of enmeshed, interdependent, and mutually defining disparate mental events (Ogden, 1986). Both sides of each polarity operate in the mind and are expressed simultaneously, albeit with different force and quality. Examples include subject/object, past/present, reality/fantasy, and sexual/spiritual. The dynamic push/pull within the psychic event of these and other polarities continuously shifts their meaning and motivational force. The flexibility of a dialectical frame allows us to move along with the constant psychodynamic motion of psychological activity, but requires an expansive, open-minded reception on the part of the analyst. Gardner (1983) echoes this sensibility when he writes that it "will do if we know that even if some of what we refer to seems only about 'inner' and some only about 'outer,' all, whether avowedly about the one or the other, is about both" (p. 18).

Dialectical attunement enhances the analyst's ability to empathically hold and reflect upon, for instance, the pain underlying the analysand's pleasure, the sense of defeat mobilized by his triumph, the hate tucked into his love, or the loss and fear stirring in his newly won sense of autonomy and freedom. The analyst's attempt to harmonize these and other such polarities, however impossible to perfect, reflects an acceptance of the contradictory, ironic manner in which the psyche functions (Lear, 2003). This sort of engagement resists simplistic either/ or thinking. Such thinking, no matter how subtle, results, to varying degrees, in either self-inflated autocratic declarations of limited or useless knowledge, or strident assertions of pseudo-ignorance and compliance. Both scenarios obscure an intolerance of not knowing that closes the mind to the complexities of life that we all, in one way or another, must contend with (see Lear, 1998, pp. 33–55).

From this perspective, the specific content of all analytic theories, while critical, is not the primary source of their explanatory power. Rather, their strength ultimately derives from their ability to move with and delineate the dynamism between the polar components of our minds and to contain the tension that arises from their clash. Analytic theories accomplish this task by constructing robust, flexible figure-ground configurations, in which, as in an optical illusion, one or the other side of the dialectic, at any one moment, appears in the foreground while the other side recesses, depending on what the analyst considers the more prominent at the time. Of course, different analytic orientations emphasize, define, and contextualize both polarities and their constituent elements somewhat differently, according to how each theory uniquely envisions reality. This will have a distinctive effect on the emotional tone and aesthetic quality of each theory, in concordance with the attributions of weightings and meanings each asserts (see Pine [2001] for a related discussion).

Schafer (1976) implies a dialectical tension, intrinsic to a mature, tragic attitude toward life, at the center of a generative analytic attitude. In contrast to the masochistic and pathetic, which insist on the possibility of "having it all" (a particular version of either/or thinking), a mature, tragic attitude understands that taking the good with the bad (and the good and bad existing *within* each other) is endemic to living. Rieff (1959) elucidates the dialectic Schafer is suggesting by noting Freud's premise that we are "not unhappy because we are frustrated . . . we are frustrated because we are, first of all, unhappy combinations of conflicting desires" (p. 343). The wisdom of a dialectical engagement is exhibited clinically through the analyst's ability to see the other side of, to empathize with, and in a balanced way to feel and think about the contradictory texture and paradoxical nature of emotional experience.

This clinical stance is authorized by an emotionally integrated understanding that a complete accommodation of the mind's incongruities is impossible; it's always a fluid, open-ended pursuit. Consequently, a search for synthesis is progressive only as an ideal to strive for, provided one does so with psychological temperance, equanimity, and, as Lear (2003) suggests, a sense of humor. Thinking dialectically resists absolutism and thereby checks against mindlessly relying on authoritarian dictate to "know" what is correct and proper.

The conceptual approach I am advocating captures the flexible manner in which mental events express simultaneously different meanings and frames of communication (Waelder, 1930; Spruiell, 1983). Psychic life involves combinations of varied aspects of experience in search of relieving compromise formations (Brenner, 1982). The multilayered, forever-mutating nature of these combinations makes them impossible to grasp from just one point of view. A dialectical understanding that can pivot in response to permutability of the patient's mental events and communications is consistent with the singular, subjective relationship with psychoanalysis—a cultivation of one's own idiosyncratic analytic style and voice—that Lear views as essential to maintaining its dynamic, forever-in-process character.

A *New Yorker* magazine article by Gopnik (2004) that remarks the resemblance between the rock musician Jimi Hendrix and the jazz guitarist Django Reinhardt illustrates this point. Gopnik writes that both "guitarists have a knack for floating in and out of styles and movements, because they are *sound makers before they are note shapers*" (p. 108, italics added). I understand Gopnik to mean that the greatness of these musicians lay in their transcending, more than most, the individual notes they played. Gopnik indicates that Reinhardt and Hendrix did not conceive of any musical note as existing as a finite objectified "thing." Notes were not, in other words, external to who they were at the moment; rather they lived through each note. For these musicians, each note was a newly created sonance that fit within the larger sound they imagined. By not getting hooked on any particular meaning of any particular note at any particular time, Hendrix and Reinhardt could engage the note open-mindedly as a subjectively created variable phenomenon—the note could flow this way and that according to the total song they were now, for the very first (and last) time, hearing in their heads.

Gopnik provides another analogy to the psychoanalytic wisdom I am attaching to dialectical thinking. He explains how both musicians addressed each note not as a single entity, but rather as an interdependent piece of a larger interlace, in tune with and in relationship to every other note of the mosaic. Like the analyst who dialectically embraces the psyche, Reinhardt and Hendrix performed with a profound apprehension of the musical experience as an entire, overall sound, a weave that's bigger than the sum of all its notes.

According to Gopnik, the genius of these musicians is defined by their in-the-moment, always-in-motion approach to their craft.

Here I am reminded of the notes of our craft—our psychoanalytic formulations, terms, constructs, clinical techniques, and interpretations. In this light, I wonder if we should be approaching the language of our psychoanalytic theories in the same way as Reinhardt and Hendrix, using them flexibly to fit each of our own unique views of the mind. Or would this, as Cooper (1988) believes, keep us too heavily immersed in the vagaries of poetry [or music], as opposed to the exactness of science? Ogden (1997), however, asserts that it would be unwise for us to objectify a lexicon when its subject matter is the evolving dynamics of a living person. His argument is worth considering:

> In attempting to capture something of the experience of being alive in words, the words themselves must be alive. Words, when they are living and breathing, are like musical chords. The full resonance of the chord or phrase must be allowed to be heard in all of its suggestive imprecision. We must attempt in our use of language, both in our theory-making and in our analytic practice, to be makers of music, rather than players of notes. To that end, we must have little choice but to accept that a word or a sentence is not a still point of meaning and will not sound the same or mean the same thing a moment later. (pp. 4-5)

dialectical thinking: Freud and Loewald

Whitebook (2004) notes the pliancy of Freud's concepts and terms that, like Reinhardt and Hendrix's musical notes, make them "overdetermined and full of connotations and implications that have not been spelled out by him or that are neglected" (p. 99). Along these same lines, Loewald (1978a) argues that:

> psychoanalysis . . . needs a less inhibited, less pedantic and narrow understanding and interpretation of its current language. Words, including concepts used in science are living and enlivening entities in their authentic function. In their interactions with "things" to which they refer, they are informed with increased or transformed meanings as these things become better known, even as words and concepts inform things with increased and transformed meaning. (p. 193)

Note the dialectic in the last sentence.

Robinson (1993) frames Freud as a "border thinker" and observes that he "is neither fish nor fowl, always at risk of being seemingly caught in a hopeless contradiction and destined to be fought over perpetually by the representatives of the two great intellectual traditions (empirical and hermeneutical) that have dominated modern culture" (p. 266). Along these same lines, Draenos (1982) sees the contradictions in Freud's metapsychology between subject and object and consciousness and matter as running through psychoanalysis like a fault line. But Draenos's more important point is that the basis of Freudian thought lies in its refusal of just these sorts of disjunctions. Draenos views these contradictions, in what he calls Freud's "mixed discourse," as the "very passageways into psychoanalysis's covert theoretical problems and novel insights; [subsequently], they are crucial to an understanding of the psychoanalytic odyssey" (pp. 7, 14 & 18).

Indeed, to my mind, the wisdom of Freud's corpus emerges from how the underlying dialectical context from which all his ideas spring gives them a resilient both/and flexibility that coheres with the dynamics of mental life. One prevalent dialectical riddle is found in his understanding of the instinctual drives as existing on the "*frontier* between the mental and the somatic" (1915, p. 122, italics added). Benjamin (1962) sees this dynamic in Freud's ideas, remarking that "the nature/nurture debate was meaningless because, for [Freud], the innate was the experiential" (p. 6). What's at stake is figuring out the intersection between the parts of human nature that are psychologically immune to the outside world (the somatic/innate) and the parts of our minds that digest external stimulation and are thereby transformed. Consider, for instance, the internal world/external reality polemic Freud (1915) is trying to resolve in the following statement about the intermingling of these two types of phenomena within the human instinct:

> [W]e may therefore well conclude that instincts and not external stimuli are the true motive forces behind the advances that have led the nervous system, with its unlimited capacities, to its present high level of development. *There is nothing to prevent us from supposing that the instincts themselves are, at least in part, precipitates of the effects of external stimulation, which in the course of phylogenesis have brought about modifications in the living substance.* (p. 120, italics added)

This nuanced supple dynamic in Freud's thinking—its dialectical wisdom—is a significant reason why his foundational notions still remain with us in so many different, ever-evolving forms. Loewald's (1960, 1978b, 1988) revisions of Freud, for example, adhere to the essentials of his outlook by similarly maintaining a robust body/mind relationship, but with a greater emphasis on human nature as intrinsically open to the external world. This enabled him to recast, in a unique way, Freud's theories of the instincts, psychological development, and analytic treatment (thus Loewald's "radical/conservative" character [Whitebook, 2004]). The connection between the two theorists, for me, stems from the way both, with equal vigor, struggle to resolve the dialectics of mental life. Despite their differences, both avoid pushing one or the other side of the psyche's experiential polarities too far out of their sight. Both see a dynamic circular movement between these polarities.

For instance, the instinctual drives are in Loewald's view still related to bodily forces, and as a consequence they retain a propulsive, physiologically based push. However, because Loewald sees the drives as organized in a human form *only* through an opening up to, an internalization of, the interaction between the maternal environment and the child, the influence of relational patterns and other external factors plays a more prominent role in his instinct concept than it generally does in Freud's. Prior to this influence, the instincts are merely potentials, "shapes, in the sense of configurations of an indeterminate degree and fluidity of organization." For Loewald, the individual's instincts "organize environment and are organized by it . . . [reflective of an] inextricable interrelatedness of the 'inner and outer' world" (Loewald, 1960, p. 23).

Loewald's (1988) privileging of interaction and internalization also extends Freud's concept of sublimation. Fluctuating between individuating from an original mother/infant unity and returning to (re-experiencing) this unity in a more differentiated and receptive mental state (able to internalize, organize, and make meaning of greater amounts of varied stimulation) becomes the sublimatory mechanism by which human beings mature as self-determined subjects. Loewald views this progressive back-and-forth movement as our natural inclination toward a "reconciliation of polarities of separateness" (1978b, pp. 23-24). Through the internalization process, the dialectics of the psyche, the mind's "higher" and "lower" elements, recombine into a novel, life-enhancing manifold that at the same time reflects the history of the individual:

> [T]he transmutations of sublimation reveal an unfolding into differentiated elements of a oneness of instinctual-spiritual experience: oneness stays alive as connection. Sublimations are progressing differentiations that culminate in new organizations of such unitary experience. . . . [B]y juxtaposing the two elements of an original unity and emphasizing the one hidden and defended against, psychoanalysis aims at showing their hidden linkage. (Loewald, 1988, p. 13)

Loewald's (1960) meditations on sublimation, his pushing Freudian concepts more toward the open-minded side of the psyche, inform his dialectical-based theory of therapeutic action that includes, but reformulates Freud's commitment to a neutral interpreter articulating objective insights to and for the patient. The analyst in Loewald's scheme represents the higher gradient (more psychologically organized, analogous to the original maternal environment) that the less integrated mind of the patient struggles to incorporate. A uniting within the patient's psyche, a meeting between her more and less organized mental elements, is set in motion. With the mediating help of the analyst's more organized grasp of the psychic flow in the analytic environment (expressed mostly through relatively objective conception and interpretation of the patient's core self, but also through silent containment of affect), these higher and lower elements within the patient reassemble. A renewed psychological structure takes shape, out of which the essential nature of the patient evolves and defines into greater relief. This process engenders an integration of something sensed as old, regained from the past, with a newly felt relatedness and the capacity for self-analysis. A firmer sense of connectedness paradoxically ushers in a deeper, stronger, and more elastic independence.

The dynamic tension created by intersecting dichotomous psychic phenomena is omnipresent in Loewald's ideas. Chodorow (2003) remarks that what drew her to his thinking is the centrality of psychic ambivalence in his view of human existence. She specifically cites his focus on the conflicting urges toward and away from individuation and primary narcissistic union (see Loewald, 1978a). This push/pull dialectic between urges for progression and urges for regression, is, according to Chodorow, the central feature of his psychoanalytic vision of humanity. Regarding the complexity and richness of human experience, Loewald (1978b) asserts:

> [We] are dealing rather with a circularity or interplay between different levels of mentation. . . . What counts is the live communication, a mutual shaping, a reciprocal conforming, of levels of mentation. The richer a person's mental life is, the more he experiences on several levels of mentation, the more translation occurs back and forth between unconscious and conscious experience. (p. 31)

Loewald takes from Freud's metapsychology a profound appreciation for the interdependent relationship between the higher (more developed and mature) and lower sides of human nature. "To make the unconscious conscious is one-sided," he writes. "It is the *transference* between them that makes a human life, that makes life rich" (1978b, p. 31). This means that to view and experience oneself and the surrounding world dialectically is to open one's mind by moderating the need for superficial black-or-white thinking. The ability to think and act wisely—to be in process of becoming a wise person—grows out of this capacity.

the clinical purpose of Freud's metapsychology: mind as both an open and a closed system

With this thesis in mind, my focus now moves to the specific manner in which Freud (1905a, 1912, 1920) attempted to synthesize in his instinct theories a metapsychological view of mind as simultaneously a closed system, fundamentally unrelated and impervious to the external world (seen clinically in Freud's original designation of transference as an obstacle to cure and later as the source of our compulsion to repeat) and as an open system inherently connected and responsive to environmental influence (transference as the path to insight and change).

The phrase that transference is both the greatest resistance in treatment and its surest conduit for psychological growth is by now so commonly accepted that we have shied away from its glaring contradiction. We no longer ask why this paradox is so endemic to analytic therapy. We no longer seem interested enough, that is, in how such a contradictory statement, one that conceptualizes our minds as both open and closed at the same time, connects with the psyche's developmental origins and evolution. I am suggesting that we reach beyond an understanding of mental life and of analytic action as always a both/and, instead of an either/or, affair. In addition, I am proposing that we turn to the *why* of mental life, that we question, for instance, whether explorations of the psyche must always be in a both/and context. If, as in the case under discussion, our minds are invariably open and closed concurrently, then why is this so?

With this question in mind, how the structural nature of the psyche manifests in the ubiquitous ironic contradictions we invariably encounter clinically becomes an overriding concern. It is to be noted that a question of this sort conceives a human reality behind and beyond consciousness. Such metapsychological speculations can't ever be captured completely or directly through self-reflection (Draenos, 1982). But any theory that includes unconscious psychodynamics, motivation, and transference repetition (reflecting autonomous psychic structure) by definition is metapsychological, in whatever form it takes. Universal essentialist assumptions about what the mind is and how it works, which involve articulating the boundaries and limits innate to our humanity, are therefore inescapable. In this way, our metapsychological thinking is in dialectical relationship to our personalized, ever-unfolding perspective on psychoanalysis. How we understand this dialectical relationship constitutes each analyst's lifework.

Addressing this dialectic from a Freudian perspective takes us into the "frontier between the mental and the somatic" (Freud, 1915, p. 122). The critical issue in this scheme is its reaching beyond the inherent openness (object-relatedness) of the neonate once it is born. Rather, Freud's metapsychological focus is related to his additional desire to explain how human beings, unlike inanimate nature and the most primitive life forms, which his adherence to Darwin led him to assume were developmentally related to people (Ritvo, 1990), went from being completely unrelated and unresponsive to environmental stimulation, to being only bodily driven and mindlessly reactive, to finally being instinctually wired toward, and able to internalize, the outside world (Dunn, 1993).

The chief tension here is the soma vs. psyche conundrum. The way Freud configured this particular dialectic may be summed up by the following question: What does it mean for human beings as psychological, meaning-making organisms to be biological (have non-mentational forces) by nature (Draenos, 1982)? All of Freud's metapsychological constructions ascend from this inquiry; he is seeking to understand mental development and functioning in terms of how the conflict between the more primitive (biological) and more mentally evolved (mentational) sides of human existence cohere and integrate. It is evident that by this question Freud is privileging the open aspects of mentality as the starting point for his inquiry. He's a psychologist of biology before a biological psychologist, but the unrelated, nonpsychological elements of human nature are not forgotten (see Draenos, 1982).

Many analysts have rejected Freudian metapsychology. They misunderstand it as a body-first approach, or they feel it loses the person as a subjective, meaning-making being and present a pseudoscientific objectification that sets the analyst up falsely as an authoritarian arbiter of reality (Klein, 1976; Schafer, 1976). While this may be so in certain instances, it need not always be the case. Metapsychological thinking, in its dialectical framework and connection with our bodily based urges, can generate deeper resonance with our more conscious psychic experiences. It gives a firm and eloquent conceptual organization of human nature with which to clinically approach our most primitive and contradictory motivations and expressions (Segal, 1993). It can keep us sharply attuned (and wise) to how daunting the task we face in trying to identify with, understand, and empathically capture interpretatively another's psychic reality that is separate and, in a most fundamental way, uninhabitable by us.

In this way, Freud's metapsychology has an inherent wisdom. As discussed above and as Loewald (1960, 1988) elaborates, Freud is trying to express and reveal the buried and obscure linkages between human beings' lower and higher sides, the instinctual and the more highly organized elements of their minds. He is providing a map for a human activity (clinical analysis) that aims to reconcile a divided mind. In other words, Freud's metapsychological insights have a functional purpose. They provide a foundational understanding of how analysts can help people feel more integrated. Said in a different way, they facilitate one's living with greater integrity, an indispensable ingredient, I believe, of wisdom.

the dialectical structure of Freud's and Loewald's metapsychology: mind as both open and closed

The tension inherent in mind's core being construed as both closed and open is one of the major conceptual tensions arising from Freud's mixed discourse in his metapsychology and clinical theory. It is, I believe, the stimulus for the misleading (because Freud's dialectics, especially those regarding body and mind, was not fully appreciated), but not unproductive debates between the adherents of the one-person, intrapsychic analytic models and supporters of the interpersonal, relational, and intersubjective orientations that have been part of psychoanalysis since its inception (Dunn, 1995; see also Gabbard, 2003).

The intrapsychic models place a heavier emphasis on the closed-off elements of the psyche. Here the mind principally functions as a solipsistic repetition of the past. Its desire inevitably must extinguish because of its inability to substantially incorporate novel stimulation into its nucleus. This concept is associated with Freud's (1905a, 1912, 1920) initial definition of clinical transference as strictly a resistance to cure as well as to his later analysis of our compulsion to repeat. This view of transference has clinical value in that it provides a means through which the analytic pair may grasp and reflect upon the analysand's fixed mental structure, what Reed (1995) terms "unconscious memory/fantasy complexes" (p. 721), since it was formed and currently exists independently of the clinical interaction.

In contrast, the open system of mental life, reflected in the intersubjective and relational models, focuses on mentation and desire as imbued with objects of the outer world. Mental life from this perspective does not repeat itself, but rather progressively transforms through continuous communication with, and internalization of, environmental forces. Herein lie the roots of Freud's (1905a, 1912) open view of transference as an essential vehicle for change. Without such an orientation, there is no basis from which to believe that analytic therapy can psychologically "enter" another human being and engender positive growth (see Bird, 1972; Poland, 1992; Lear, 2003; Loewald, 1960, 1986).

In terms of Freud's instinct theory, this duality began with his posing the drives, on the one hand, as the "most abundant sources of internal excitation originating in the interior of the body" (1920, p. 34), and on the other hand, as the "psychological representatives" of such somatic, non-mentational stimuli (1915, p. 122). Freud's primary concern in the former statement is establishing a biological grounding for psychic life. His focus is on the body-based drives, the sense of the push, rather than the meaning, of our activity. Here, he is theoretically committed to the non-mentational physical nature of the source and aim of the drive, viewing the object to which it is attached as secondary because of its relative externality to our biophysiology (Freud, 1905b, 1915). Freud, however, reverses himself by also considering the drives as constituted by our capacity to symbolize physical sensation. Instincts are now mental phenomena related to the body, but not bodily in themselves. And, as they are psychic in character, they are innately made up of, and operate in coordination with, environmental forces and interactions.

Freud's (1920) struggle to reconcile the contradiction between mental life as an open versus a closed system appears in sharper focus in his later instinct theory, where he replaces the sexual and aggressive drives with the life and death instincts. No longer is it bodily fuel that drives our psyches, nor psychic representatives of our bodily states; instincts are now forces permeating animate nature, dynamic urges that regulate the way our minds naturally work (Lear, 1996).

Influenced by the temporally based Darwinian evolutionary context, Freud (1938) characterizes our death instincts as regressive, pulling us backward with a final aim to "lead what is living into [its native] inorganic state" (p. 148). As such, the death drive embodies the part of our minds that propels us to resist external influence. Here we are compelled by nature to shut ourselves off from the life of the outer world and to return to the nonexistence from which we originally came. And this requires an innate drive to destroy all pre-existing structures of life.

In contrast, Freud's Eros is the aspect of mind that opens up to life. It drives us to communicate and join with all that is outside of ourselves. Rather than destroying what has been built up, its forward-moving aim is to "establish even greater unities and to preserve them" (Freud, 1938, p. 148). From an evolutionary point-of-view, its purpose is to continue life. This urge reflects our innate, instinctual capacity for openness and change through the internalization process that Loewald highlights.

As psychoanalysis comprehends the psyche as a totality, bigger than the sum of its parts, the dichotomy between the closed system (Thanatos) and open system (Eros) represents dual aspects of this totality. Dissimilar in character but still related, each pole plays an interdependent and reciprocally influential role in mental functioning. Psychic growth obviously requires openness. But we must also simultaneously separate and establish boundaries by retaining stable, self-enclosed internal images and organizations—maintain, that is, a mind of our own (Caper, 1997). To develop a sense of who we are, we must feel ourselves existing as a separate reality in other people's minds. That is, we form our identities partly by seeing ourselves through the eyes of the other, and this development—this establishing an inner and outer self with borders separating us from the outer environment—requires the other to be experienced as external to the subject (Spezzano, 2007). This idea underlies Loewald's (1960) belief in the therapeutic necessity for the analyst to maintain and indirectly communicate a flexible, yet sturdy, internally enclosed image of the patient's potential, what he could be in the future, but doesn't yet realize—an aspect of the developmental "gradient" (see Cooper, 1996).

In this context, it is interesting that Freud (1920) hints at, but discards, a more complex backward-forward/open-closed conception of Eros. There is a suggestion that, within Eros, alongside its outward and forward motion toward life, there exists, as within Thanatos, a regressive urge that shuts off the mind and destroys. This would mean that an open vs. closed dialectical tension exists within Eros. Given Freud's evolutionary perspective, this assertion would make sense. Seeing Eros, life, as emerging from inanimate substance infers that it would, as a secondary force, retain the closed-off, regressive characteristic of that substance—the death drive—from which it came. Rudimentary relics of a death instinct would be a constituent force in our drive for life.

Loewald's treatment of Eros illuminates this dual character. He sees, within Eros, an urge to mentally close off by moving backward toward a non-self experience within the primal maternal bond (a "oneness") from which we were born. "Subject-object differentiation is suspended [in this mental state] . . . and if not tempered by secondary process and object love, leads to chaos and self-destruction" (1978b, pp. 41-42). However, within this same regressive urge of Eros, Loewald also posits an antithetical forward movement of the mind that opens up to and internalizes life that is external to itself. This engenders a more highly developed and complicated form of psychological experience. There is a "fresh unity [being] created by an act of uniting, [so that] . . . in this restoration of unity there comes into being a *differentiated* unity . . . that captures separateness in the act of uniting and unity in the act of separating" (pp. 23-24).

In other words, we go backward to go forward, which Cooper (2000) identifies as a regression-progression tension in Loewald's view of the therapeutic action of interpretation. The commonsense wisdom here is that in order for a person to evolve into something else, she must have some impetus to dismantle her already existing structure. Loewald (1979) explicates this point when he describes how in human development there is a psychical, but no less real, destruction, a real killing-off from one generation to the next. His point is that to individuate and grow we must continually destroy and then remake the internal parental objects that we've established in our minds.

Loewald's (1978b) emphasis on Eros is about recreations into psychological health that emerge from mutually enhancing joinings of different modes and levels of our psyches. Approaching these elusive mutualities, these unified internal experiences, requires an increasingly robust capacity of our minds to incorporate elements from the external world and to make this new life a part of our own minds.

wisdom, dialectics, and open-mindedness in clinical work

The metapsychological ideas I have presented about wisdom, dialectical thinking, and open-mindedness are easily grasped as an academic exercise, but to put this into practice in one's life and analytic work is an entirely different matter. Life experience is required to develop the emotionally integrated understanding that makes dialectical thinking in Freud's and Loewald's metapsychology genuinely useful as a human activity and mode of communication. In *The New York Review of Books* Sue Halpern (2005), reviewing Elkhonon Goldberg's book *The Wisdom Paradox*, supports this idea from a neuroscience perspective: "The exposure to similar, new things creates neural networks in the brain that attract each other and accumulate . . . The networks accrue with age—Goldberg ventures to call the result of this accumulation wisdom—and are, therefore, unavailable to young people" (p. 20).

These comments bring me back to Lear's (2003) concern that psychoanalysis thrives only by every analyst's forging for herself a personal, self-defined relationship with psychoanalysis. To me this means that for a paper on wisdom (or any other psychoanalytic issue) to be relevant, it can't avoid getting personal. All psychoanalytic discussions, by their very nature, arise from the thinker's desire to understand and improve herself. Explorations of analytic ideas are most meaningfully addressed when they germinate from an introspective reflection that involves a basic question: What is it about me, my innermost life, that is inquiring about this particular subject in the particular ways that I am (Lear, 2003)?

A genuinely meaningful response to this question takes time and effort. I trace my own interest in wisdom and dialectics to when I was in graduate school 25 years ago, about the time I first imagined myself as a psychoanalyst, a persona I idealized because it seemed synonymous with being a wise person. In one class, the teacher began by asking: Does the patient come to analysis to get better, or does he come to defeat the analyst's efforts to help him get better? I don't remember the class's reaction, but I do recall that my teacher made no further comments and that I was left weighing one side of this question against the other for many years to come in an effort to find the right answer.

I am no longer looking for this right answer in that I don't believe one exists in the way that I used to. I have come to realize what anathemas such either/or approaches are to psychoanalysis—and I have become increasingly sensitive to how subtly present and active such thinking is in our literature and public presentations. Nevertheless, my interest in this question hasn't waned. The reasons for this, as far as I know them, have everything to do with my desire to explore and understand the relationship among wisdom, psychoanalytic theory, and analytic therapy from which I can grow.

These thoughts relate to my earlier comments about Loewald's views of therapeutic action. He believed that analysis's potential to promote psychic growth in the patient's core emerged through the development of more differentiated, complex intrapsychic and interpersonal integrations. This view implies that analytic treatment is an interaction in which an internal process of self-becoming—or in Freud's (1933) words, "where id was there ego shall be" (p. 80)—takes place and that the analysand is his own agent of change. The value of the analyst's ideas, from this perspective, do not revolve around their objective-truth value, rather around their capacity to stimulate the patient to arrive at and articulate truths that genuinely generate from within him (Ogden, 2003, 2004).

The therapeutic effects of the relational currents flowing between the analytic pair, as opposed to the content of the analyst's interpretations, are critical to this analytic process as is the quality of the analyst's narcissistic investment in his ideas (see Wilson, 2003). The analyst's capacity to fine-tune, calibrate, and in many cases suspend his need to assert authorship of the analytic process goes hand-in-hand with his openness to the fact that he is always, to a large extent, operating in the dark and on the basis of what he doesn't know (Grossman, 1999). Wisdom here manifests as the ability to show that one can live comfortably, and with an open mind, with what one doesn't know and cannot do.

In this design, the analyst's interpretations—what he actually *tells* the patient— fades to the background, while the surrounding clinical atmosphere from which the analyst's indirect influence arises—what the analyst *shows* to the patient through his mode of communication—comes to the fore. Lear (2003) picks up on this idea by stressing the greater significance of the "how" (the form of communication) as compared to the "what" (the content of the interpretation) in our clinical interactions. Because the how immediately becomes a what at the point that the analyst informs her patient directly about her (the analyst's) mode of communication, the therapeutic influence of the how obviously must reach the analysand through the backdoor, through the cracks in the overt clinical dialogue.

Along these same lines, Loewald (1975) suggests that everything said by the analyst to the patient overlays a deeper meaning that is being communicated. Elsewhere he (1980) speaks of the "global nature of [the analyst's] personal presence and the likelihood that such presence involves more than the usually listed perceptual and communicative modalities" (p. 286). "The analyst's therapeutic art," Loewald explains,

> does not consist in mere reporting to the patient what the analyst perceives and how he interprets it but . . . in the analyst's capacity and skill of conveying to the patient how he, the analyst, uses his own emotional experiences and resources for understanding the patient and for advancing the patient's access to his, the patient's, inner resources. And there may be at times, in addition, that other quality to the analyst's communications, difficult to describe, which mediates another dimension to the patient's experiences, raising them to a higher, more comprehensively human level of integration and validity while also signaling the transitory nature of human experience. (p. 82)

I emphasize this particular figure-ground configuration (form over content) of therapeutic action because analysts lose whatever therapeutic effect their wisdom may have once they try to directly spell it out to the analysand, i.e., those who tell others that they are wise are betraying just how foolish they really are. Here I am reminded of a story I grew up with. It begins with a young farm boy asking his idealized neighbor how he may get the big muscles he's wished for ever since he saw the strongman perform at the circus. The neighbor tells the boy that he'll think about this question, but in the meantime the boy should go around back and chop some wood. At the end of the day, the neighbor tells the boy he hasn't yet found the answer, but that the boy should come back tomorrow. The boy returns the next day, and the neighbor tells him the same thing as he did the day before: to chop some wood while he searches for the solution to the boy's problem. This pattern repeats itself day after day; the boy keeps chopping wood because he believes that eventually the neighbor will figure out how he can get big muscles. And, of course, after two months of chopping wood, the boy, while remaining completely unaware that the neighbor has shown him the answer to his problem, has developed muscles that are beyond his wildest dreams.

The neighbor in my story conveyed his wisdom indirectly. What are the chances the boy would have sustained the rigors of chopping wood every day for two months if the neighbor told him point-blank that this was the way to get big muscles? Similarly, I imagine that the analyst's wisdom stirs the patient almost as if by osmosis, making itself known not only in the overt verbal communication and the content of the interpretation itself, but also in the background attitude and sensibility of the analyst (Lear, 2003; see Schafer, 1983).

These considerations raise the forever-to-be-debated question: How do we keep an open-minded receptivity to who the analysand is and, at the same time, effectively tell the analysand what we "know" about him? Put another way, How do we assert our desire to inspirit our analysands' minds with our ideas, with who and what we are, and not, in so doing, close ourselves off to the analysands' natural desire to do the same with us, to influence us and reside in our minds, to become who they naturally are?

For example, the neighbor in my story held back whatever inclinations he had to play the "wise man who knows" of the boy's fantasies, and instead put himself in the background. In this way, he redirected the boy's fantasy of passively receiving big muscles into a self-directed active pursuit of his own. Be that as it may, despite his deft handling, the neighbor's influence was very much at the center of the boy's mental activity. The neighbor was indirectly but surely asserting something of himself. In his actions, he was displaying what he knew of the boy in particular, of boys of that age in general, and of the culture they both inhabited. His loving desire to help the boy, his wisdom regarding how to reach and motivate him must also have been evident, but in a way that defies a clear understanding of its progressive mechanism.

The question of how analysis facilitates psychic growth, how one person affects another for the better, leads me to another question posed by Lear (2003): How do we write about or in other ways teach psychoanalysis psychoanalytically? Here my teacher's either/or challenge is relevant. The fact that never receiving a direct answer from him was instrumental in finding one for myself is a clue to one way of responding to Lear's question. At the time I did not know that my teacher's question had started me on a path of thinking about wisdom in psychoanalysis in ways unique to who I am and reflected in the type of self-inquiries that make sense to me. How I developed and grew from this pursuit was embedded in my seeking, but not finding the answer I originally thought I was after. This relates to my previous citation of Lear's belief that all psychoanalytic topics, to be meaningfully addressed, must begin with an introspective self-reflection into the personal reasons for one's curiosity, choice of topic, and method of inquiry. To my mind, a necessary wisdom is built into this approach to learning, teaching, and writing psychoanalysis. Lear's method recognizes the personal, subjective basis of all our knowledge. However, we must also consider how this understanding coheres with the need for us to maintain some baseline metapsychological assumptions about the universality of human nature that transcend the individual, another essential component of our analytic work. Whatever the answers we arrive at, a dialectical engagment with this and other questions embraces, rather than repels the tension arising from the indeterminability of all our knowledge about mental functioning and about analytic treatment. Holding this tension in the forefront of our minds keeps our minds as open as possible. And here a final dialectic of this paper emerges, namely, the irony that psychoanalytic inquiry into ourselves, beyond anything else we do as analysts, facilitates our ability to sensitively and generatively engage with others.

references   Benjamin, J. D. (1961), The innate and the experiential in child development. *Lectures in Experimental Psychiatry*. H. W. Brosin, ed. Pittsburgh: University of Pittsburgh Press.

Bird, B. (1972), Notes on transference: universal phenomenon and hardest part of analysis. *Journal of the American Psychoanalytic Association,* 20:267–301.

Brenner, C. (1982), *The Mind in Conflict.* New York: International Universities Press.

Caper, R. (1997), A mind of one's own. *International Journal of Psychoanalysis,* 78: 265–278.

Chodorow, N. J. (2003), The psychoanalytic vision of Hans Loewald. *International Journal of Psychoanalysis,* 84:897–913.

Cooper, A. M. (1988), Our changing views of the therapeutic action of psychoanalysis: comparing Strachey and Loewald. *Psychoanalytic Quarterly,* 57:15–27.

Cooper, S. (1996), Facts all come with a point of view. *International Journal of Psychoanalysis,* 77: 255–274.

Cooper, S. (2000), *Objects of Hope.* Hillsdale, NJ: The Analytic Press.

Draenos, S. (1982), *Freud's Odyssey: Psychoanalysis and the End of Metaphysics.* New Haven: Yale University Press.

Dunn, J. (1993), Psychic conflict and the external world in Freud's theory of the instinctual drives in light of his adherence to Darwin. *International Journal of Psychoanalysis,* 74:231–240.

Dunn, J. (1995). Intersubjectivity in psychoanalysis: a critical review. *International Journal of Psychoanalysis,* 76:723–738.

Freud, S. (1905a), Fragment of an analysis of a case of hysteria. *Standard Edition.* London: Hogarth Press, 7:1–122.

Freud, S. (1905b), Three essays on the theory of sexuality. *Standard Edition.* London: Hogarth Press, 7:125–245.

Freud, S. (1912), The dynamics of transference. *Standard Edition.* London: Hogarth Press, 12:97–108.

Freud, S. (1915), Instincts and their vicissitudes. *Standard Edition.* London: Hogarth Press, 14:109–140.

Freud, S. (1920), Beyond the pleasure principle. *Standard Edition.* London: Hogarth Press, 18:3–64.

Freud, S. (1933), New introductory lectures on psychoanalysis. *Standard Edition.* London: Hogarth Press, 22:1–182.

Freud, S. (1938), An outline of psycho-analysis. *Standard Edition.* London: Hogarth Press, 23:141–207.

Gabbard, G. O. & D. Westen (2003), Rethinking therapeutic action. *International Journal of Psychoanalysis,* 84:823–841.

Gardner, M. R. (1983), *Self-inquiry.* Boston: Little Brown and Company.

Gopnik, A. (2004), Gypsy. *The New Yorker,* 80(38): 102–108.

Grossman, L. (1999), What the analyst does not hear. *Psychoanalytic Quarterly,* 66:84–98.

Halpern, S. M. (2005), The moment of truth? *The New York Review of Books,* 52(7):19–21.

Klein, G. S. (1976), *Psychoanalytic Theory: An Exploration of the Essentials.* New York: International Universities Press.

Lear, J. (1996), The introduction of eros: reflections on the work of Hans Loewald. *Journal of the American Psychoanalytic Association,* 44:673–698.

Lear, J. (1998), *Open-minded: Working Out the Logic of the Soul.* Cambridge: Harvard University Press.

Lear, J. (2003), *Therapeutic Action: An Earnest Plea for Irony.* New York: Other Press.

Loewald, H. W. (1960), On the therapeutic action of psychoanalysis. *Papers on Psychoanalysis.* New Haven: Yale University Press, 1980.

Loewald, H. W. (1975), Psychoanalysis as an art and the fantasy character of the psychoanalytic situation. *Journal of the American Psychoanalytic Association,* 23:277–299.

Loewald, H. W. (1978a), Primary process, secondary process, and language. *Papers on Psychoanalysis.* New Haven: Yale University Press, 1980.

Loewald, H. W. (1978b), *Psychoanalysis and the History of the Individual.* New Haven: Yale University Press.

Loewald, H. W. (1979), The waning of the Oedipus complex. *Papers on Psychoanalysis.* New Haven: Yale University Press, 1980.

Loewald, H. W. (1980), Psychoanalytic theory and the psychoanalytic process. *Papers on Psychoanalysis.* New Haven: Yale University Press, 1980.

Loewald, H. W. (1986), Transference-countertransference. *Journal of the American Psychoanalytic Association,* 34:275–287.

Loewald, H. W. (1988), *Sublimation: Inquiries into Theoretical Psychoanalysis.* New Haven: Yale University Press.

Ogden, T. (1986), *Projective Identification and Psychoanalytic Technique.* Northvale, NJ: Aronson.

Ogden, T. (1999), On the art of psychoanalysis. *Reverie and Interpretations: Sensing Something Human.* Northvale, NJ: Aronson.

Ogden, T. (2003), What's true and whose idea was it? *International Journal of Psychoanalysis,* 84:593–606.

Ogden, T. (2004), An introduction to reading Bion. *International Journal of Psychoanalysis,* 85:285–300.

Pine, F. (2001), Listening and speaking psychoanalytically— with what in mind? *International Journal of Psychoanalysis,* 82:901–916.

Poland, W. S. (1992), Transference: "an original creation." *Psychoanalytic Quarterly,* 61:185–205.

Reed, G. S. (1995), Clinical truth and contemporary relativism: meaning and narration in the psychoanalytic situation. *Journal of the American Psychoanalytic Association,* 43:713–739.

Rieff, P. (1959), *Freud: The Mind of the Moralist.* New York: Viking Press.

Ritvo, L. B. (1990), *Darwin's Influence on Freud: A Tale of Two Sciences.* New Haven: Yale University Press.

Robinson, P. (1993), *Freud and His Critics.* Berkeley: University of California Press.

Schafer, R. (1976), The psychoanalytic vision of reality. *A New Language for Psychoanalysis.* New Haven: Yale University Press.

Schafer, R. (1983), *The Analytic Attitude.* New York: Basic Books.

Segal, H. (1993), On the clinical usefulness of the concept of death instinct. *International Journal of Psychoanalysis,* 74:55–61.

Spezzano, C. (2007), A home for the mind. *Psychoanalytic Quarterly,* 76:1563–1583.

Spruiell, V. (1983), The rules and frames of the psychoanalytic situation. *Psychoanalytic Quarterly,* 52:1–33.

Waelder, R. (1976), The principle of multiple function. *Psychoanalysis: Observation, Theory, Application.* E. A. Guttman, ed. New York: International Universities Press.

Whitebook, J. (2004), Hans Loewald: a radical conservative. *International Journal of Psychoanalysis,* 85:97–115.

Wilson, M. (2003), The analyst's desire and the problem of narcissistic resistances. *Journal of the American Psychoanalytic Association,* 51:71–99.

3263 Sacramento St., Suite C
San Francisco, California 94115
jondunn567@aol.com

Freud's and Loewald's metapsychologies **Jonathan Dunn**

When cultures collide: myth, meaning, and configural space*

Marilyn Charles

This paper explores the relationship between cultural myths and clinical experience. The author makes use of individual case material to exemplify the way that culture informs the development of primary and secondary processing as it is elaborated in dream work, and thus in the space of the psychoanalytic session. Looking at the case of a man whose history is nested in both Eastern and Western culture serves to illuminate not only the individual dilemma, but also the transformative and obfuscating functions of the unconscious processes themselves.

Human experience is far more complex than we can ever fully comprehend. As we wrestle with complexity, we run up against the limits of mind and imagination and develop various systems for representing and communicating our experiences. In developing models as ways of organizing and simplifying meanings within a conceptual frame, we risk losing sight of the whole (Matte-Blanco, 1975), creating an ongoing dialectic in which we are always up against partial truths. We can augment our understanding to the extent that we can encounter other "truths" and reflectively consider and attempt to integrate them. Toward this end, it is useful to have some awareness of the strengths and vulnerabilities governing and constraining our enquiries. My own particular sensibilities have lent themselves to an interest in patterned nonverbal experiences and in how these patterns provide conceptual anchors that guide meaning and desire (Charles, 2002a, 2004). This interest finds fertile ground in psychoanalysis.

*This paper is an expanded version of a colloquium given at the Emory University Psychoanalytic Studies Program, Atlanta, Georgia, April 5, 2007.

Freud's model of psychoanalysis is based on his insight into how meanings are conveyed through the dreamwork, much as anthropologists use myth and other narrative traditions as models through which to understand the work of culture. These models have in common the provision of a structural framework that helps us to envision the formal interrelationships among elements in dimensional or "configural" space. Configural space is a useful rubric for conceptualizing multiple relationships between forms—a strategy that is particularly important when investigating the complexities of psychic reality. As we come up against the limits of our capacity to hold in mind complex webs of interrelationships, we need models that can assist us in reflectively considering not only the interplay among elements, but also how these relationships change over time.

Having this type of underlying structure in which to embed our experience and to thereby organize the various facts at our disposal may be particularly important in psychoanalysis, an endeavor that requires that we venture out beyond the known onto an uncertain edge of experience. In this work, we are continually challenged to keep one foot on whatever ground we can find while also finding our bearings in psychic reality. That uncertain edge is the point at which we can begin to find an other as other rather than as a reflection of our own projections. In spite of our ability to articulate psychoanalytic concepts, it is easy to overlook their manifestations as they occur in daily life. Transference, for example, is endemic in human relationships, and the unconscious *is* unconscious. We can catch glimpses of the unconscious through its effects but, by definition, can never quite see it directly. If we believe in the subject as in some sense uniquely unknowable, our work entails moving beyond the known into a space of uncertainty, much as we invite the analysand to venture out beyond the constraints of her own certainties (Levinas, 1999).

Acknowledging our limits—and thus also our ignorance—affirms our willingness to learn about whatever eludes us because it flies below our radar or because we've picked up a danger signal and instinctively veered away. This acknowledgement models to the patient a belief in rewards that accrue from an inquiry into unknown territory rather than affirming a belief in acquired knowledge that can be passed along directly from teacher to student or from doctor to patient (Charles, 1998, 2004). In this precarious juncture in which the analyst is relatively blind to the particulars of the other's individual experience but knows something of the path to be traversed, much of what the analyst accesses is stored in the unconscious, in implicit memory, as opposed to being more directly accessible to the conscious mind. At times, the only anchor in moments of uncertainty is whatever feels true in the moment if we can also keep in mind a sense of the particular ways in which our own defenses and transferences tend to skew our perceptions. If we can speak from our own experience, and also listen respectfully to the other, we can sound the distance between and thus gauge our progress and perhaps catch glimpses of what eludes us.

The psychoanalytic journey requires that each participant try to sit with painful feelings, taking note of ways in which we resist and defend, and inquiring into the dark spaces of whatever remains unknown or unconsidered. One hazard is presuming sameness or difference in ways that obscure the particularities of an individual life. In some ways, what is marked as *other* is easier to inquire into, whereas apparent sameness can provide a slick surface that is difficult to penetrate. As Bion (1977) notes, focusing on the process by moving to the level of configural structure can help us see beyond aspects of content that can obscure the functional relationships. Shared preconceptions can easily become invisible, making it important to have some external reference point—some "third"—by which to recalibrate or re-evaluate alliances, allegiances, and other potentially pathological certainties as they become fixed (Muller, 2007; Shapiro, 1982). It is language, for Lacan (1977a), that cuts into our grandiose, omnipotent fantasies, forcing us to contend with the inevitability of limits, as the mother "names" the father, the third vantage point that breaks into the symbiotic dyad and thus comes to represent law and the demands of the social order.

As we move beyond the dyad and try to orient ourselves in the complicated arena of interpersonal relations, we have various ways of marking what is other and what is not. Each designation is both a useful point of orientation and also to some extent a lie. For example, it is convenient to have diagnostic labels that mark the outer bounds of reality and the beginnings of some other way of being that is sufficiently alien to be denoted as "psychotic" even though we also know that the psychotic marks realities that can be quite uncanny in their acuity but stand outside of conventional agreements regarding what might be noticed or spoken about. We also come up against these tensions around issues of culture, where self and other may be arbitrarily defined by race, religion, or the color of one's skin, and consensual agreements regarding acceptable behavior may vary widely.

As mentioned previously, sameness can cloud our ability to detect difference, while difference obscures the ability to note similarities of meaning that define and circumscribe the worldview (Matte-Blanco, 1975, 1988). The Oedipus complex, for example, has been termed a universal dilemma, and yet there are differences across cultures in terms of the force, potency, or valence of the dilemma. For example, whereas Freud focuses on incest, others suggest that confrontation with authority is of greater primacy. Bion (1977) pulls back from this apparent dichotomy to envision the larger configural frame. From this vantage point, he describes the underlying dilemma in the oedipal tale as similar to other myths (such as the story of the Garden of Eden) in which it is willful blindness that is at issue, a willful blindness in which each individual can find himself implicated.

In these tales, we can see the importance of what has been termed the "third" or the "name-of-the-father" in locating knowledge or truth beyond either the individual or dyadic perspectives, and also in affirming the importance of language as a symbolic function that anchors meanings, thus providing a protection against empty speech (Lacan, 1953/1977). Such an external reference point helps us to obtain a clearer distinction between the universal and the particular, thereby also providing some distance from our preconceptions through which to more reflectively consider the positions we take and thus, perhaps, to catch a glimpse of our own "pathological certainties" (Shapiro, 1982).

If our preconceptions or received knowledge has not been challenged by or integrated through personal experience, we are not well prepared to grapple with puzzles and problems as they present themselves. Following Freud's (1916, 1966) statement to Lou Andreas-Salomé, Bion (1990) suggests that if we are to attempt to understand obscure subjects such as "the most fundamental and primitive parts of the human mind . . . instead of trying to bring a brilliant, intelligent, knowledgeable light to bear on obscure problems," we should instead "bring to bear a diminution of the 'light'—a penetrating beam of darkness; a reciprocal of the searchlight" (p. 20). Bion likens this discipline to the task of observing a game of tennis being played in the dark, suggesting that if we can tolerate watching in the darkness, we might be able to stop looking for the net and see, instead, the "holes, including the fact that they are knitted, or netted together" (p. 21). If we can accept our ignorance and accustom ourselves to the darkness, he suggests, the object of our attention might reveal itself to us as it absorbs some of the light that surrounds it, rather than being overshadowed by our brilliant illuminations.

Looking at the holes, as Bion proposes, encourages us to tolerate our ignorance rather than trying to immediately overcome it. When dealing with unconscious defenses, which by definition resist our efforts to detect them in ourselves, it may be essential to have in mind a model that encourages us to hold steady when we would most like to leap away. As we will see in the case example, the capacity to be present under duress can be a major factor in one's ability to learn from the experience of the moment in the service of one's own development. Having in mind that there is always a larger perspective from which a situation might look different from what we currently see or imagine it to be helps us to enquire into the darkness of what is not yet known, rather than accepting presumed knowledge in a way that occludes further understanding or exploration. While collisions between opposing viewpoints can be uncomfortable, they also serve as signals of a gap that might be attenuated through further enquiry.

Bion (1977) notes the utility of dual vantage points—"binocular vision"—in illuminating complex dilemmas. As we consider what becomes opaque when viewed through the lens of a given culture, a comparison of alternative mythic frameworks can be particularly useful in highlighting commonalities and differences. Levi-Strauss (1984) stresses the importance of multiple vantage points in appreciating cultural differences, suggesting that in order to understand universal problems, one must be able to look from both inside and out in order to see "what is peculiar to each culture in the form of myth, ritual and language—that is, in domains where the oppositions are both identifiable and unconscious" (p. 22).

meaning in time and space

Much as Bion (1990) points to the holes that can be discerned if we attend to the associative links, Lacan (1977b) picks up on a theme originally introduced by Freud (1924) to note that it is in the space beyond what initially captures our attention that significance is revealed. Ricoeur (1970), conceptualizing the work of culture in line with the dreamwork, suggests that hidden desire can be located through the ways in which it is disguised within a given frame, that is, we use symbolic forms to render more visible whatever is most difficult for us to tolerate knowing. In the words of Ricoeur: "Psychoanalysis is of value insofar as art, morality, and religion are analogous figures or variants of the oneiric mask. The entire drama of dreams is thus found to be generalized to the dimensions of a universal poetics" (p. 162). The mask helps titrate the distress.

Adding insights from Melanie Klein to our understanding of the formal structures of the unconscious, Obeyesekere (Molino, 2004) describes the unconscious as "inhabited by *beings*, and not just drives and wishes" (p. 55), so that "narrativization, the very act of telling a story about illness may itself be part of the cure" (p. 58). Through the study of dreams, we see how meanings can be anchored in the positioning of subjects and objects in relation to one another (Charles, 2003). Narrative, then, provides a structure that helps us track transformations of these relationships across time. Ricoeur (1984) points out that as a "transcultural form of necessity . . . *time becomes human to the extent that it is articulated through a narrative mode, and narrative attains its full meaning when it becomes a condition of temporal existence*" (p. 52).

Time, therefore, is essential to meaning, providing an anchor in configural space for the primary perceptual elements that speak profoundly and directly and thus *insist* on recognition. This is the realm of myth in which universal truths are located in relation to an ethos framed by culture (Charles,

2004). For Cassirer (1957), it is in myth that we find the purest representations of symbolic form, in that "the world of mythical experience is grounded in experiences of pure expression rather than in representative or significative acts" (p. 68). In his terms, the myth has something of the form of a hologram, in which the parts contain the whole rather than the whole being capable of division into substantive parts. In line with current understanding of the crucial organizing functions of affect in human memory, Cassirer anchors meaning in affect, suggesting that it is in the embodiment of affect that meanings can be perceived. This perspective is affirmed by research that shows that such meanings are embedded in the prosody of visual and auditory manifestations of affect that are taken in directly without requiring conscious thought (Stern, 1985). In Cassirer's words, "the expressive meaning attaches to the perception itself, in which it is apprehended and immediately experienced" (p. 68).

The narrative form of myth provides a containing structure through which universal feelings might be comprehended by bringing them into, as Cassirer (1957) puts it, "a kind of spiritual focus, into the unity of an 'image'" (p. 108). Because images arise directly from affect, they are by nature ephemeral and so it is the representation of the image that enables it to persist, both as a single instance and also as a symbol for something greater from which the instance emanates. These representations are then linked through the containing structure of the myth, which, like the dream work, derives meanings through spatial relations (Charles, 2003). Cassirer (1957) notes: "Myth arrives at spatial determinations . . . by lending a peculiar mythical accent to each 'region' in space, to the 'here' and 'there,' the rising and setting of the sun, the 'above' and 'below'" such that each region has definitive meanings, cloaked and vivified by their magical, mystical significance (p. 150). Language then provides a structure through which these meanings persist and thus can be rediscovered. Language, Cassirer observes, "provides that possibility of 'finding-again' and of recognition by virtue of which totally different, spatially and temporally separate, phenomena can be understood as manifestations of one and the same subject" (p. 108). What Cassirer is describing is the ability to detect patterns—or as Bion (1965) calls them "constant conjunctions"—and to build a narrative that makes sense within the meanings defined and proscribed within the frame of a given culture.

If we think of Cassirer's notion of the realm of myth as one in which meanings are defined and organized in terms of spatial relationships within a conceptual order, we can see how elusive it might be to attempt to define these meanings for one who is so deeply embedded in the culture that the road signs are implicit and thereby not easily noted. We can also imagine the complications for one who is *not* deeply embedded in the cultural order of his origins and yet is affected by meanings derived from that culture. Psychic reality is such that our conceptions of self, other, and universe are informed by the conceptions of those around us, even if these are not consciously known or communicated.

In deference to the precarious nature of "meaning," Bion (1977) developed his model of psychoanalytic inquiry using Poincaré's idea of the selected fact to reference the powerful effects of perspective on how we organize information. Coherence is always in relation to whatever selected facts are organizing the frame, and content can obstruct our ability to take note of whatever underlying factors are at play. Bion's (1989; Charles, 2002b) grid provides a structural model through which to view process, structure, and functional relationships abstracted from the obfuscating effects of content. If we see Freud's model of psychoanalysis as built on an enquiry into that which is explicitly not known but becomes revealed because it can be sufficiently displaced, disguised, or negated, then we can see that the grid anchors this task by pointing us toward the relationships themselves that can remain obscured when we focus on content.

Bion (1977, 1989) was acutely aware that any action could be used toward development or evasion, and so, using his grid as a model of the analytic process, he locates a given statement or interaction in terms of the complexity of the thought, the sophistication of the thinking, and the function being served. In Bion's schema, myth holds a privileged position as a model that helps to anchor and give form to subtleties of experience. He was aware that "facts" are artifacts of the particular cultural and personal lenses though which they are viewed. By using the grid as a rubric through which to note constant conjunctions, he hoped "that the selected fact, that gives coherence and relatedness to the hitherto incontinent and unrelated, will emerge. Thus 'nominated,' 'bound,' the psycho-analytic object has emerged. It remains to discern its meaning" (1963, p. 103).

From another perspective, the meaning comes to our attention as we stumble over a gap that indicates that something is missing. For Lacan, the gap announces an absence that could be meaningful if we are able or willing to notice. He suggests that this gap does not merely signify a failure to attend, but rather an alienation or denial of meaning, which he terms "aphanisis" (1977c, p. 210). This alienation from and denial of meaning seems similar to what Bion (1967) describes as an "attack on linking," through which process an associative link is denied, thereby de-signifying an element of experience that might otherwise carry significance.

case study

If we think of culture as defining selected facts and of myth as a containing structure within which facts might reveal latent meanings through the use of symbols in relation to one another, we can begin to consider the plight of an individual whose history is located in two disparate cultures. To illustrate my topic, I'll use the case of a young man whose reality is configured in relation to two mythic histories: one, the country of his birth, and the other that of his parents' birth. His life journey has taken him back and forth between two continents with different underlying mythic structures. Our work together has required an enquiry into the overlay between cultures as we try to understand the interplay between our shared culture and the underlying Hindu myths, symbols, and traditions that inform my patient's narrative. The transparency offered through these dual vantage points helps us to notice the configural elements, rather than being blinded by the opaqueness of whatever remains unnoticed because it is too similar or too different from the cultural signposts we share.

If we also look through two lenses of theory, keeping in mind both Bion's grid and Cassirer's (1957) ideas regarding the "revolution" that takes place in the transformation from "action to schema, to the symbol, to representation" (p. 153), we see how each of these men anchored thinking in perceptions embedded in primary affective experience. What I like about pairing these two minds is that, in the spirit of what Bion (1977) refers to as "binocular vision" and the "confluence of the senses," we can see how each of these thinkers was working on a common dilemma, i.e., how a consideration of dream, myth, meaning, and culture can inform our understanding of this basic human process of utilizing configural, affectively driven meanings in the service of greater understanding or potency in our ability to navigate in our lives.

Mr. A's dual citizenship affords the greater transparency of binocular vision through which to consider collisions between frames of reference and how these collisions may become more transparent so that we can better recognize ways in which we stumble into them and perhaps more effectively come to grips with our own preconceptions. The differences between Hindu and Western mythologies offer an opportunity to note the slightly different flavor of the confrontation with the Third between these two cultures, thus perhaps illuminating our larger enquiry. This confrontation with the Third is represented in what has come to be seen as the oedipal dilemma. For psychoanalysts, this myth captures the multiple difficulties encountered by the young child who must face the limits of his or her omnipotence and also the limits of the exclusivity of the relationship with the mother.

Mr. A was born in the United States, but was deeply affected by his parents' conceptions of culture and reality, which continue to be prescribed and circumscribed by the myths, mores, and symbolic traditions of their native India. For Mr. A, the process of narrativization is obscured in conflicting veils of a palimpsest of intertwining cultures, further complicated by traumatic memories that distort his perceptions. An enquiry into his inner life, mind, and being is essentially an enquiry into the otherness that is an intrinsic fact of his reality from which he cannot escape. As he struggles with this issue of otherness, the twin poles of his reality twist and turn like a Möbius strip with two sides that can neither be clearly seen nor distinguished from one another. This blurring of the edges in some ways offers respite from his fear of seeing more clearly exactly what he fears finding in himself. The failure to notice the gaps between meanings as represented by one culture versus the other has resulted in my patient's being unable to understand himself or to make sense of his relationships with others. Feeling caught by others rather than being able to locate himself in relation to an other has resulted in his fighting off seemingly imminent destruction in the face of any approach. He finds himself jumping away from whatever seems treacherous or alternatively becoming so sleepy that he cannot consciously attend to the source of his discomfort. His defenses work so well that it is only by taking note of them in retrospect that he can begin to approach the subject of his unconscious desires.

In my work with Mr. A, his dreams have anchored his dilemmas in ways I could not make sense of from the plethora of detail he puts before me in our sessions. I experience his talking as the type of "empty speech" Lacan (1977c, 1977d) refers to, speech that marks the place of something that cannot be directly articulated. Empty speech, Lacan suggests, skims over the surface, leaving virtually no ripple. The absence of meaning can be difficult to discern in the moment, thus inviting the clinician to fail to recognize the meaninglessness that has been introduced, and introducing a note of perversity into the therapeutic dyad. The perverse element can be seen as an invitation to the clinician to "miss" something in the patient and to overlook problems, likely reenacting the absent or neglectful parent. In such circumstances, being able to notice what is missing can be crucial, pointing to the possibility of a different type of relationship in which the patient can count on the vigilance of the therapist to be alert for information that is not easily accessible to the patient. At times, what is missing may be communicated nonverbally by the patient through the patterning of elements in relationships or in dreams. These patterns provide conceptual anchors that help us to organize and reorganize our thinking. Analysts often find that patients offer up a dream that anchors the essential elements of the life story and, with it, of the dilemma at hand. This was the case with Mr. A. I will briefly describe the treatment, offer a few snippets of dreams, and then discuss the dream that seems to contain the essentials of this man's life story.

Mr. A is a 36-year-old man who has the appearance and demeanor of someone much younger. He is currently in his third year of medical school. Both parents are from southern India, each deeply embedded in the cultural traditions of their home-land. Mr. A has unhappy memories of summers in India with his family, feeling constrained and bored, longing to return home. In many ways he is caught between two cultures, not comfort-able in either, searching for home. In Indian culture, distinc-tions between parent and aunt or uncle, sibling, and cousin are not the same as in western culture. His childhood narrative is peopled by an extensive network of relationships in which desig-nations were not clear and boundaries were often transgressed. One maternal uncle, in particular, is marked as a predator in the family. Mr. A experienced this uncle as extremely abusive and became immersed in the discipline of Aikido as a way of denying and managing his feelings of vulnerability.

Mr. A left home early, trying to find a place for himself in the country of his birth. A dark-skinned young man in urban middle America, he felt most at home with the rough-and-tumble youth from the inner city, who also felt themselves to be at the margins of society. In his adolescence, Mr. A's world was shaken by the attempted suicides of the two female cousins who appear in the dream that will be discussed here. In the wake of these events, he discovered that the same uncle who had tormented him was also implicated in his cousins' distress. These cousins each took their stand at the point at which a marriage had been arranged for them. As Mr. A describes it, the family turned a blind eye to the various ways in which these young women attempted to signify their pain: one shaving her head; the other running away. A third cousin did actually commit suicide during the same year in which Mr. A's father was diagnosed with dementia and his college men-tor (who had become like a father to him) was diagnosed with cancer. These three events resulted in a tailspin that interrupted Mr. A's medical school dreams at that time. The reasons for the cousins' despair could not be discussed, and the father became enraged whenever Mr. A tried to talk with him about his illness. Mr. A felt even more alienated from his family as he attempted to grapple with these events alone. There seemed to be important meanings that could not be signified in this family.

Mr. A first sought treatment with me three years ago, in the context of a failed love relationship and the impending deaths of his father and his longtime college mentor. The mentor had recommended that he seek treatment, likely recognizing the tremendous vulnerability of this traumatized young man. Initially Mr. A was living in a nearby town, and we met in person. But when he was away at school, we held our sessions by telephone, meeting in person when he could do so. The frequency of sessions varied from four to five times per week.

Mr. A is extremely likeable. His ready smile and earnest attention invite a sense of engagement that is belied by his descriptions of being ever ready for the next attack. In the countertransference, however, one can easily mistake one's emotional responsiveness to the stories he is telling as marking Mr. A's own ability to empathically engage with these traumatic memories. Mr. A entered treatment believing that, somehow, he would tell a story that would serve whatever purpose had been defined and then quickly be on his way. What he encountered instead was some recognition, at the level of primary sensory experience, of the extent of the troubles he faced, including his desire to cut and run, to close up this hole he had created in his own story of seamless self-sufficiency.

In the first month of treatment Mr. A reported a series of dreams that proved to be important metaphors, reminding me that this young man who represented himself as thoroughly embedded in our shared American culture also had deep roots in his southwest Indian heritage. These dreams provided anchors in configural space that became more fully elaborated over time, guiding our work together. In the first dream, a dust bunny he is prodding with his toe turns into something living—a rodent, then a cry-baby lion cub that reminds him of the Lion King dying to protect his son from the uncle—but then it is eaten by a hamster. He shows it to his mentor's wife and then it becomes a wet Kleenex that reminds him of a toilet that links in turn to a sexual predator and then to being rescued when chased by wild dogs in the Himalayas.

The following day he returned to this dream, associating to the comic books of his childhood, one in particular of Shiva's dreadlocks being cut and falling to the floor, becoming an army of demons. He then associated to his uncle's ridiculing his tears, calling it "pissing through your eyes." From there, his thoughts went to having tried to talk to his cousin M as an adult, only to have her sister K bar the way as if *he* were the predator.

Two weeks later, Mr. A reported the dream that will anchor the treatment. He described being in a woods on a well-worn path, four feet across. There is dirty water, like a swamp, on one side with trees growing out of it and a hill on the other side. There are three or four dilapidated, barn-like structures in a series on the hillside of the path. On each end there is a structure. On one end there is a medical school though he never quite sees it. He's walking to or from the other end, where there is another dilapidated wood building that he only sees once. There's a bird in a birdcage hanging over the path. The cage is rusty. The bird is a brilliant white blue, and it is observing things.

Elaborating on the dream, Mr. A says:

> The colors are all grey except the bird. The only other person is my cousin M and her sister K—there's evidence that she is there. I'm staying in one of these barns; there's a dirt floor and I feel safe in the daytime. In the morning, I follow M to her med school class. As she's walking, she is wearing a vest and reaches down into the water. She takes a few sips, shrugs as though the water is dirty. I say, "Isn't it dirty?" but she doesn't answer. Then she keeps going, and I lose sight of her because she goes into the med school. I remember feeling very alone. I turn and walk down the path. Day is ending and it is getting darker. There's a sense of panic. I can't get to where I sleep. There's a lack of light. Her place is absolutely uncomfortable, but it's closer. I find the place where she stays. It's creepy, an old barn with a dirt floor. I look down and our dog is next to me. I lock the door just in time. It's sunset. I see freshly raked dirt. There's a rusty bike covering a quarter of the freshly raked part, lying across on a diagonal. I can see the dog, so I feel better, and I can feel that this is where K and M speak.

Mr. A talks about lying nestled in the place where they had been. At a later point in time, we return to this moment:

A: I'm thinking of your dream again—the parrot, which seems to represent your Indian heritage on the one side, and the med school on the other, and the place where you nestle in between.

P: D [his mentor] knows a lot about Indian culture. Even in India he's my comfort zone. He helps me become calm again.

A: There was something in the dream about laying where comfort had been . . .

P: Yeah, it was warm. There was still the imprint of where her body had been and it was very comfortable. . . . . . This bird— it seems like there's a whole segment that occurs before I'm following M. I'm walking down the path and I see the bird—it's eerie. I'm not supposed to show it—something—I need to keep something hidden.

I ask him about his associations to the bird, and he talks about a bird in his childhood home.

> He's old. Whenever someone didn't want their pet, we got him. This bird watches everything, and if you're eating and he wants it, he makes a fuss until he gets some. Once I threw a pen at him, and he didn't forgive me for ten years, but he has a close relation- ship to my dad, and my uncle could trim his beak. I suspect it has something to do with that I was keeping things hidden from my dad and mom. It wasn't malicious; I just wanted them to ask me directly. The bird was hanging slightly over, so it could see the path. I feel like this has something to do with my dad. He's a doc- tor. Seeing down the path to the med school. Both K and M went to med school. I lost touch with them.

In my work with Mr. A, I have had a strong sense that his life nar- rative is embedded in both his adopted and ancestral cultures and that the meanings of the symbols he brings into our work are occluded by our joint difficulty in unpacking the meanings of these symbols and thereby anchoring them in the structure of his life. This sense is affirmed by the enactment in his cur- rent life of this very confusion. Mr. A has found a non-Indian "family" who, through their entrenchment and deep interest in India and its religious and mythic structures, translate to him his underlying culture through the reassuring remoteness of the lens of the culture in which he was raised. In educating me about some of the meanings of these symbols and struc- tures and his relationships to them, Mr. A helps to build a con- ceptual map through which I help him to locate himself. In counterpoint, I am able to view the complex interrelationships between the two cultures in a way that invites some transpar- ency through which, as Bion terms it, I can begin to see the spaces that hold the net.

Mr. A offered me a hint of the divergent paths of oedipal de- velopment in India—and of aspects of his own developmental dilemmas—when he left me a small statue of Ganesha, the re- mover of obstacles and the god of all beginnings. Apparently, as another patient who noticed the small statue later told me, Ganesha should never be procured directly for one's self but rather should only be received as a gift. In giving me this gift, Mr. A both endorses me as a "remover of obstacles" and locates in my consulting room the otherness in which he is embedded.

Kakar (1989), following Bose, suggests that the oedipal dilemma is not as strong in Indian culture as in Western culture because the desire to be female is less ego-dystonic. In Indian culture, according to Bose, "The Oedipus mother is very often a combined parental image," lending itself to greater "fluidity of . . . cross-sexual and generational identifications" (qtd. in Kakar, p. 355). The dominant narrative of Hindu culture, in terms of male development, is not that of Oedipus, but rather of "Devi, the great goddess, especially in her manifold expressions as mother in the inner world of the Hindu son" (p. 356).

One manifestation of Devi is as the mother of Ganesha and Skanda. Whereas Skanda is handsome and heroic, Ganesha, born solely of his mother, was beheaded by his father, who, realizing his mistake but unable to locate the boy's head, found instead an elephant's head to place on the boy's body. "Iconically represented as a pot-bellied toddler with an elephant head and one missing tusk," as Kakar (1989) explains, "he is represented proportionately as a small child when portrayed in a family group" (p. 358). For Kakar, "Skanda and Ganesha are personifications of the older child on the eve of the Oedipus complex. He is torn between a powerful push for independent and autonomous functioning and an equally strong pull toward surrender and re-immersion in the enveloping maternal fusion from which he has just emerged" (p. 359). Whereas in Western culture Skanda would be enviable, in Indian culture it is Ganesha who has the preferred position. At the price of remaining an infant, he does not have to feel the pain of separation from the mother.

In Mr. A's culture of origin, parental ties are more complex and diffuse than in Western culture. He did not have merely two parents, but rather grew up in a web of relationships with cousins and aunts and uncles whose roles were not clearly differentiated from those we would term the "nuclear family." For example, the mother's brother lived with the family through much of Mr. A's childhood. Whereas the father was experienced as warm and approachable to the young child, but then became painfully out of reach, this uncle was omnipresent as a harsh, critical, and attacking figure. The mother's role, in my patient's mind, was to not-know what was not convenient to know and to attempt to manipulate her son into whatever path or action she desired, in line with cultural traditions.

Going back, then, to the parrot dream, having in our minds both Skanda and Ganesha, we can locate Mr. A on a journey from a resting place where warmth had been, on a road that had been foreclosed (he cannot go back to the place he began, yet at the same time he never quite reaches the goal). He rests for a while in a place where there had been the yearned-for closeness from which he had felt barred (the world of his female cousins, which he describes as very intimate) and tries to follow his cousin but cannot. There is no resolution in the dream between the desire for a preoedipal union with the parent and the inability to go back to his origins or reunite with his cousins. In Mr. A's associations, nestling only occurs in relation to a paternal figure; the maternal figure is alternatively engulfing or withholding.

The paternal function, in contrast, seems to offer greater hope although it is still not clear how one would make the journey to adulthood. The bird seems to both point and bar the way, much as the road to medical school had been pointed to by both his uncle and his father: his father in expectation; his uncle in derision. There is no solid ground under Mr. A's feet; the earth as he treads it reminds him of an experience on a rain forest path, where he had felt a particular springiness to his step—as though the earth were not quite solid. In this image, one feels the layers of history in varying stages of decay yet each fragment retaining aspects of the former whole.

In this particular dream element, we find Mr. A feeling through the layers of his history and prehistory, searching for tolerable meanings but fearing the intolerable. This bind between hunger and fear is present throughout the dream as he seeks out but never actually makes contact with another human being. This same ambivalence was particularly salient in the early months of our work together as he moved back and forth between his longings for the father whose genes he carries and his reliance on the other father, a professor of Indian studies, who had adopted not only him but his culture of origin. The former was dying of Alzheimer's, and the latter of cancer. Mr. A came to me so squeezed between their impending deaths that he could barely pause long enough to think. Much of our preliminary work entailed discovering the underlying fears so that they could be tolerated and explored, whereas later work required moving further into the configural aspects of the myths that underlie and prescribe meanings in this man's universe. The co-existence of two disparate cultures both complicates and eases our path, as the very complication forces us to look more explicitly at the myths themselves. As we recognize these cultural gaps, we are more open to enquiring into whatever lies beyond the story being told. At that point, what has tended to recede as background and become invisible becomes more highly illuminated—or, in Bion's terms, darkened—such that we can begin to see the threads of meaning entangling Mr. A.

These threads became an important metaphor recently as he continued to note and struggle with his tendency to "jump"— to become distracted and move forward. For example, if he hit something difficult to take in while reading, he would jump ahead without realizing what he'd done, resulting in empty spaces or gaps in his knowledge. Eventually, it was the gaps that caught his attention, alerting him to his own defenses. In looking back at the spaces that had become gaps, he could see that these were emotionally laden, and he could better catch his defenses in action. Together, we form a metaphor of how he jumps over what seems too difficult, leaving, however, a thread behind such that as he continues to jump, the web of threads grows, like a spider web in which he gets caught again and again, becoming hopelessly entangled without any idea why. The ideas have been left behind in the spaces, as noted in his dream, where the affective meanings have nestled. He longs for these affective ties but so fears becoming entangled in them that he jumps as soon as the discomfort arises.

Behind him we begin to discern (as we are less blinded by the light he shines to ward off the recognition he fears will be vilifying) the web closing in, choking and strangling him more and more tightly in the very moment of running away as his defensive maneuvers enable him to elude any real intimacy with other human beings. He begins to see how he attempts to create longing in the other as a way of not being the one left longing. What he cannot yet do is tolerate meeting desire with desire. That still seems too treacherous. We come up against images of the engulfing mother, and that is where we find Devi, who can create life and take it away and who, at some level, commands even the great god Shiva.

Early in Mr. A's treatment, we could understand that he had been terribly traumatized by the lack of empathic engagement by his parents and the relatively unchecked abusiveness of his uncle. What was less evident, however, but became clearer through his dreams and through the stories he would tell, were the deeper meanings of this web of interrelationships and how these configured an idea of self in relation to others and to the universe that was absolutely intolerable. In his dreams, we could better see how the myths of his parents' homeland were alien, but also fundamentally entangled in his own worldview.

Perhaps most stunning in Mr. A's dream is the absolute isolation. The only person mentioned in the dream does not answer him when he speaks to her, but rather disappears, leaving only an empty space where he nestles to find some warmth, some comfort. Even the bird does not speak to him, but rather seems to guard a path that closes in as the dream progresses. In Mr. A's depiction, there had been no one to help him make sense of all the bits of experience he could not usefully link together. Now he and I sit with the silence amid the multiplicity of words and try to build a narrative in which he can learn to sound the darkness and also encounter real others without such idealization, demonization, or terror that he must flee blindly, leaving larger and larger gaps where connections might have been.

Through his dreams, Mr. A brings me up against the edge of what he consciously knows and allows me glimpses of aspects of his experience that he cannot yet integrate. In coming up against this edge, I stumble over what appears familiar to me (looking for love), and what is not (thinking about prospective partners as an amalgam of qualities one might consider in an arranged marriage). As I speak to him of this stumbling, he can, in turn, begin to glimpse the gap between what he consciously believes about himself and those factors lying underneath that have been hidden from view. Learning to keep in mind the both/and as opposed to the either/or of his experience is helping him to appreciate these dual cultures that are each alive and well within him. This appreciation enriches his experience and affords him better grounding as he travels a path rife with layers of history and prehistory. As he learns to integrate disparate aspects of self, he finds himself on a road increasingly peopled by individuals whose qualities he can better recognize and differentiate. Misunderstandings can be considered rather than requiring immediate defensive maneuvers, and problems can conceivably be worked through.

Dreams call to us, in part, because they lull us with their sense of intrigue and mystery. With our defenses softened in this way, we can better tolerate knowing a bit more of what we fear and how we fend off the very understanding that might help us better make our way in the world. Mr. A's dreams both obscure and reveal his dilemma. As one colleague suggested to me, in some ways Mr. A's dreams become a version of Scheherazade's *One Thousand and One Nights* as he fends off his own beheading at my hands by weaving beautiful, vibrant stories for me. And yet, the very vibrancy of his tales reminds me that his spirit is steeped in a tradition different from mine, one of vibrant colors and multiple gods. His flying carpet is both an evasion and a definitive statement. For just as surely as he is desperately trying to evade the intolerable, he is also working at trying to make it tolerable. Like all of those who seek psychoanalysis, what is needed is to encounter someone with sufficient faith in this possibility to enable the seeker to tolerate the journey required to achieve it.

references   Bion, W. R. (1963), *Elements of Psycho-Analysis*. London: Heinemann.

Bion, W. R. (1965), *Transformations: Change from Learning to Growth*. London: Tavistock.

Bion, W. R. (1967), *Second Thoughts*. London: Heinemann.

Bion, W. R. (1977), *Seven Servants: Four Works*. New York: Jason Aronson.

Bion, W. R. (1989), *Two Papers: The Grid and Caesura*. London: Karnac.

Bion, W. R. (1990), *Brazilian Lectures*. London: Karnac.

Cassirer, E. (1957), *The Phenomenology of Knowledge*. Vol. 3 of *The Philosophy of Symbolic Forms*. London: Oxford University Press.

Charles, M. (1998), On wondering: creating openings into the analytic space. *Journal of Melanie Klein and Object Relations*, 16(2):367–387.

Charles, M. (2002a), *Patterns: Building Blocks of Experience*. Hillsdale. NJ: The Analytic Press.

Charles, M. (2002b), Bion's grid: a tool for transformation. *Journal of the American Academy of Psychoanalysis and Dynamic Psychiatry*, 30:429–445.

Charles, M. (2003), Dreamscapes: portrayals of rectangular space in Doris Lessing's *Memoirs of a Survivor* and in dreams. *Psychoanalytic Review*, 90:1–22.

Charles, M. (2004), *Constructing Realities: Transformations through Myth and Metaphor*. Amsterdam: Rodopi.

Freud, S. (1916), Letter from Freud to Lou Andreas-Salomé, May 25, 1916. *International Psycho-Analytical Library*, 89:45.

Freud, S. (1924), Neurosis and psychosis. *Standard Edition*. London: Hogarth Press, 19:147–154.

Kakar, S. (1989), The maternal-feminine in Indian psychoanalysis. *International Review of Psycho-Analysis*, 16:355–362.

Lacan, J. (1953), The function and field of speech and language in psychoanalysis. *Écrits*. A. Sheridan, trans. New York: W. W. Norton.

Lacan, J. (1977a), Of the subject of certainty. *The Four Fundamental Concepts of Psycho-Analysis*. A. Sheridan, trans. New York: W. W. Norton.

Lacan, J. (1977b), The Freudian unconscious and ours. *The Four Fundamental Concepts of Psycho-Analysis*. A. Sheridan, trans. New York: W. W. Norton.

Lacan, J. (1977c), The subject and the other: alienation. *The Four Fundamental Concepts of Psycho-Analysis*. A. Sheridan, trans. New York: W. W. Norton.

Lacan, J. (1977d), The subject and the other: aphanasis. *The Four Fundamental Concepts of Psycho-Analysis*. A. Sheridan, trans. New York: W. W. Norton.

Lévi-Strauss, C. (1984), *Anthropology and Myth*. Oxford, U.K.: Basil Blackwell.

Levinas, E. (1999), *Alterity and Transcendence*. M. B. Smith, trans. New York: Columbia University Press.

Matte-Blanco, I. (1975), *The Unconscious as Infinite Sets: An Essay in Bi-Logic.* London: Duckworth.

Matte-Blanco, I. (1988), *Thinking, Feeling, and Being: Clinical Reflections on the Fundamental Antinomy of Human Beings and World.* London: Routledge.

Molino, A. (2004), *Culture, Subject, Psyche: Dialogues in Psychoanalysis and Anthropology.* Middletown, CT: Wesleyan University Press.

Muller, J. P. (2007), A view from Riggs: treatment resistance and patient authority-IV: why the pair needs the third. *Journal of the American Academy of Psychoanalysis and Dynamic Psychiatry*, 35:221–241.

Obeyesekere, G. (1990), *The Work of Culture: Symbolic Transformation in Psychoanalysis and Anthropology.* Chicago: The University of Chicago Press.

Ricoeur, P. (1970), *Freud and Philosophy: An Essay on Interpretation.* New Haven: Yale University Press.

Ricoeur, P. (1984), *Time and Narrative.* Vol. 1. K. McLaughlin & D. Pellauer, trans. Chicago: The University of Chicago Press.

Shapiro, E. R. (1982), On curiosity: intrapsychic and interpersonal boundary formation in family life. *International Journal of Family Psychiatry*, 3:69–89.

Stern, D. N. (1985), *The Interpersonal World of the Infant: A View from Psychoanalysis and Developmental Psychology.* New York: Basic Books.

25 Main Street
P.O. Box 962
Stockbridge, MA 01262-0962
mcharles@msu.edu

When cultures collide: myth, meaning, and configural space **Marilyn Charles**

Rereading narcissism: Freud's theory of male homosexuality and Hawthorne's "Gentle Boy"

David Greven

The author examines Freud's theory of narcissism and homosexuality in the context of Hawthorne's "Gentle Boy." In this reading, the problematic but conceptually intriguing notion of narcissism as at the root of male homosexuality is explored through the lens of Hawthorne's characterization, and addressed in relation to psychoanalysis and queer theory.

In their recent study *Sexual Orientation and Psychodynamic Psychotherapy*, Richard Friedman and Jennifer Downey (2008) challenge the uses of Freud's theory of the Oedipus complex for the pathologization of homosexuality. Traditionally, deviations from the normative resolution of the Oedipus complex, such as homosexuality, have been diagnosed as pathological forms of the complex and therefore of properly heterosexual adult sexuality. Friedman and Downey, making note of "profound change[s] in psychoanalytic theory in recent years in the areas of sexual orientation," argue that, contrary to classical psychoanalytic thought, "superego development, gender identity, sexual orientation, personality structure, the etiology of the neuroses (and the psychoses)—all seem to be subject to influences other than oedipal conflict resolution or failure thereof" (p. 97). Salutary though their revisionist work proves to be for new, antihomophobic psychoanalytic methods of interpreting the dynamics of gay identity in a rapidly changing world, that the authors dispense entirely with narcissism—a crucial aspect of Freud's thinking on homosexuality and, indeed, within his thought generally—in their reassessment of classical psycho-analytic theory and survey of new approaches seems to me a disturbing and worrisome error.[1]

The opprobrium narcissism has historically elicited—from its endurance as a cautionary tale throughout Western literature to its familiar usage as a pejorative assessment of an overly prideful character—intersects with the psychoanalytic diag-nosis of narcissism as pathological. In this essay, I reexamine Freud's thinking on narcissism, particularly as it pertains to homosexuality, in order to challenge the prevailing deroga-tions of narcissism and to make the case that narcissism re-mains central to any theorization of desire. I also mean to recuperate the role narcissism plays in Freud's theory of ho-mosexual childhood development. My project proceeds from the theoretical, rather than clinical, dimensions of psycho-analysis, and any attempt to rethink narcissism, I believe, has to take into account that pathological forms of it do indeed exist in severe mental illness, such as schizophrenia and other forms of psychosis. Less severely, but nevertheless painfully, the narcissism of intensely self-involved persons for whom an obsessive interest in the self damagingly limits their emotional lives and intersubjective relationships must be understood as problematic, as a barrier between satisfying relationships with self and other.

The figure of the homosexual narcissist, who could also be described as the narcissistic homosexual, recurs throughout Freud's work. Within queer theory—the methodology that informs my argument—great controversy over the Freudian view of homosexuality endures. While many have contemned Freud's theory of homosexual narcissism as pathologizing and inherently homophobic (Warner, 1990; Fuss, 1995), others have found enough complexity in Freud's thinking on the subject to use his work not for the purposes of further pathologizing ho-mosexual narcissism, but instead, to enlarge our view of desire and to use psychoanalysis to challenge homophobic thinking

---

1 Whereas voluminous entries in the index refer to the Oedipus complex, not a single one points to narcissism. Although Friedman and Downey's dis-cussion of the mother-child relationship is relevant for our study, they are not sufficiently attentive to narcissism as its own profound category in phenom-enological considerations of desire and identity.

(Dean, 2001; Lane, 2001; Bersani, 2001). The present essay proceeds from this latter line of thought.

The historical psychoanalytic pathologization of the narcissistic identity has hit homosexuals with particular force. Psychoanalysis has contributed to the pathologization of homosexuality generally—not consistently, to be sure, but nevertheless demonstrably—and the pathologization of narcissistic personality, both analogous to and constitutive of the pathologization of homosexuality, carries with it the double vexations of psychoanalytic homophobia, even as homophobia can be thoroughly challenged *through* psychoanalytic means. So my effort to recuperate narcissism as a positive—if unstable and ever-fraught—category of identity necessarily involves a challenge to this homophobia, albeit a challenge that emerges from within a psychoanalytic project; moreover, it also demands an effort to recuperate Freud's view of homosexuality as narcissistic.

Freud's theory of homosexual narcissism is only one piece of his larger thinking on narcissism. The narcissist and the homosexual are sometimes indistinguishable from each other in Freudian thought; but in the ways that they are indeed distinct, they nevertheless always double each other as "perverse" forms of identity. Moreover, they have consistently, as types, been broadly used as embodiments of the same negative character traits: obsessive if not pernicious self-involvement, an inability to love, arrested development, a hatred of the opposite sex, a deep and abiding penchant for surface rather than depth. In order to make a case not only for the radicalism that inheres in Freud's theory of homosexual narcissism, but also the plangency, I will consider narcissism more generally as Freud describes it in his 1914 essay on the subject, "On Narcissism: An Introduction." I will demonstrate that narcissism is just as integral to Freud's view of heterosexuality as it is to homosexuality, and I will present the idea that the value of Freud's theory of homosexual male narcissism lies in its generally resonant interpretation of the mother-son bond. In conclusion, I will turn to the work of one of the most Freudian of American writers, Nathaniel Hawthorne, the subject of a classic Freudian study by the literary critic Frederick Crews (1989). (Crews famously repudiated Freud and his own Freudian study of Hawthorne.) I will make the case that it is Freud's theory of narcissism, rather than the oedipal paradigms Crews employs, that most acutely illuminates Hawthorne's writing. The Hawthorne work that I will discuss, "The Gentle Boy," bears a striking resemblance in its thematic concerns to Freud's treatment of the homosexual child. In bringing these works together, I will establish that Freud illuminates precisely the aspects of Hawthorne's work that come closest to making a political statement about the ways in which males are socialized generally in Western patriarchy. More deeply still, both Freud and Hawthorne provide us with profound insights into the experiential and social experience of maternally identified and narcissistically inclined male desire.

Before turning to "On Narcissism," however, it is important to consider some of the reasons why Freud remains for many a deeply problematic figure in terms of efforts to challenge homophobia because in my view Freud is, on balance, a thinker who challenges sexual orthodoxies rather than establishes them; it is with his controversial theorization of homosexuality that his not unproblematic, but nevertheless important theorizations of same-sex desire properly begins.

homosexuality, perversity, homophobia

In his aversive Foucauldian reading of Freud, Michael Warner (1990) argues that the concept of narcissism has been "primitively" used in psychoanalytic theory to calumniate queer sexuality as regressive and self-fixated (pp. 190-207). The most useful point of his argument is his challenge to the view prevailing in some circles that the homosexual narcissist desires himself reflected in someone else, that he desires sameness. "Why is gender assumed to be our only access to alterity?" Warner heatedly asks, "Can it actually be imagined that people in homosexual relations have no other way of distinguishing between self and not-self? That no other marker of difference, such as race, could intervene; or that the pragmatics of dialogue would not render alterity meaningful, even in the minimal imaginary intersubjectivity of cruising?" (p. 200). Warner then declares that

> The central imperative of heterosexual ideology is that the homosexual be supposed to be out of dialogue on the subject of his being. Imagining that the homosexual is narcissistically con-

tained in an unbreakable fixation on himself serves two functions at once: it allows a self-confirming pathology by declaring homosexuals' speech, their interrelations, to be an illusion; *and more fundamentally it allows the constitution of heterosexuality as such.* (p. 202)

Warner wants us to understand that psychoanalysis, as an arm of power, facilitates the "utopian erotics of modern subjectivity" that works to obscure what institutionalized heterosexuality has in common with homosexuality, a dependence on "a self-reflexive erotics of the actual ego measured against its ideals," a dependence made visible in homosexuality but decisively obscured in heterosexuality. "Heterosexuality deploys an understanding of gender as alterity in order to mobilize, but also to obscure" what are its own "narcissistic sources," hence the crucial function of a "discourse about homosexuality as a displacement" of these disavowed sources (1990, p. 206).

I'm in full agreement with Warner about the primitiveness of a view of homosexuality that reduces it to desire for sameness and as a stunted inability to recognize and erotically respond to "difference." Yet the central flaw of Warner's powerful argument is that it hinges on a reductive and unimaginative reading of Freud, whose conceptualizations on this score are actually complex, unpredictable, and suggestive. Freud returned to the subject of homosexuality several times, sometimes seeing it as one of the perversions, sometimes as the "most important of the perversions" (cold comfort, to be sure), but his attitude was not one of "condescending" hostility, as Warner describes it (1990, p. 193). How "inappropriate to use the word perversion as a term of reproach," he writes in "Three Essays on the Theory of Sexuality" (1905, p. 160). Freud clarified that perversions become pathological when they assume "the characteristics of exclusiveness and fixation" (p. 161). It is the later uses made of Freud, especially in American psychiatry, that have emphasized the pathological nature of the perversions. All of this is to say that in calling homosexuality a perversion, Freud was not pathologizing it in the manner of later psychiatric treatments; Freud found homosexuality a richly suggestive and disturbing site of inquiry, and his treatment of it cannot be simply dismissed as phobic.

The most surprising omission in Warner's critique of Freud's views on homosexuality is the centrality of the mother-son relationship to Freud's theory of homosexual development. In a footnote added in 1910 to his "Three Essays on the Theory of Sexuality," Freud (1905) conjectures that homosexual identity emerges from an identification with the mother:

> In all the cases that we have examined we have established the fact that the future inverts, in the earliest years of their childhood, pass through a phase of very intense but short-lived fixation to a woman (usually their mother), and that, after leaving this behind, they identify themselves with a woman and take *themselves* as their sexual object. That is to say, they proceed from a narcissistic basis, and look for a young man who resembles themselves and whom *they* may love as their mother loved *them*. Moreover, we have frequently found that alleged inverts have been by no means insusceptible to the charms of women, but have continually transposed the excitation aroused by women on to a male object. They have thus repeated all through their lives the mechanism by which their inversion rose. Their compulsive longing for men has turned out to be determined by their ceaseless flight from women. (p. 145 fn. 1)

This theory has proven extremely contentious and controversial, and in my treatment of it, I do not seek to exculpate Freud for the aspects of his argument that lend themselves to homophobic views. What I do wish to suggest here is that, however perniciously exploited as a basis for homophobic practices at certain points of the history of American psychiatry, Freud's theory of the mother-son relationship in terms of homosexuality should not necessarily be treated as itself pernicious; at the very least it should be reexamined.

The sheer range of cultural myths about the male homosexual encapsulated in this passage from "Three Essays" staggers the mind: male homosexuals and their mommy fixation; male homosexuality as narcissistic self-love; male homosexual desire as desire for sameness—for the replica of the self (they "look for a young man who resembles themselves"); homosexual desire as an expression of panic over female sexuality; homosexual desire as a substitute for normative heterosexual desire; homosexual desire as a kind of repetition-compulsion through which some form of sexual trauma can be relived, reexperienced, but never resolved ("repeated all through their lives," "their compulsive longing"); male homosexuality as an attempt to escape women ("ceaseless flight"). What is truly staggering about this passage—only a footnote—is its prescriptive power, the extent to which it managed to install a particular set of images about male homosexuality in the popular imagination.[2]

Warner leaves something else out of his discussion of Freud's view of homosexuality as a perversion: the centrality of perversity to Freud's thinking, and both homosexuality's and heterosexuality's relationship to it. As Dollimore (1991) points out in his superb treatment of Freud in *Sexual Dissidence,* "Freud described homosexuality as the most important perversion of all," and "as the most repellent in the popular mind," while also being "so pervasive to human psychology" that Freud made it "central to psychoanalytic theory" (p. 174). If the value of psychoanalysis lies in its exposure of the essential instability of identity, Dollimore writes, "then this is never more so than in Freud's account of perversion. At every stage perversion is what problematizes the psychosexual identities upon which our culture depends" (p. 181).

In Freud's (1905) own words:

> a disposition to perversions is an original and universal disposition of the human sexual instinct . . . normal sexual behaviour is developed out of it as a result of organic changes and psychical inhibitions occurring in the course of maturation . . . Among the forces restricting the direction taken by the sexual instinct we laid emphasis upon shame, disgust, pity, and the structures of morality and authority erected by society. (p. 231)

In Freud's most famous formulation, the Oedipus complex eradicates the infant and young child's access to polymorphous pleasure, properly socializing us to desire normatively by identifying with the same-sex parent and desiring the other who resembles the opposite sex parent (part of socialization is the prohibition on both homosexuality and incest). If socialization buries our polymorphous perversity under repressive decorum, perversity is only buried, not eradicated; and what keeps it bur-

---

2 Charles Socarides, for example, was a pioneer in the movement to "cure" homosexuality through psychiatry. As Bayer (1987) notes, Socarides was to become, "in the late 1960s and early 1970s, a leading and forceful proponent of the view that homosexuality represented a profound psychopathology" (p. 34). In Socarides' own words, "Homosexuality is based on fear of the mother, the aggressive attack against the father, and is filled with aggression, destruction and self-deceit. It is a masquerade of life in which certain psychic energies are neutralized and held in a somewhat quiescent state. However, the unconscious manifestations of hate, destructiveness, incest and fear are always threatening to break through" (qtd in Bayer, p. 34).

ied, what constitutes repression, are an odd assortment of "social dams," such as the curious triumvirate of shame, disgust, and pity.

For Freud, the oedipal conflict arises in both genders: in boys, the male child's arousal of sexual feelings in the form of erotic attraction to the mother and the arousal of aggressive, violent feelings in the form of sexual rivalry with the father whom he wishes to supplant; in girls, a variation of these themes, but also an essentially perplexing and mysterious process that Freud nevertheless subjects to numerous theoretical reformulations. Once it is successfully resolved, however, we are purged of our wild, uncontrollable polymorphous-perverse energies. [3]

The successful resolution of the oedipal conflict is identification with the dominant parent (the father) and realization that while erotic fixation on the mother prepares us for sexual object-choice, it must cede to exogamous sexual affiliations: the mother is not to be sexually desired and the object of desire must be outside the family. The Oedipus complex effects

---

3 Freud remains one of the most controversial analysts of sexuality, especially when it comes to the discussion of female sexuality. Freud's difficult treatment of the oedipal complex for girls remains deeply controversial. Without discounting the problems of Freud's sexism, I would argue that he exposes the effects of misogyny at the same time as he constructs them. In his 1925 essay "Some Psychological Consequences of Anatomical Distinction between the Sexes," Freud explores masculine and feminine identities within patriarchy. Writing of penis-envy—a theory that can only be recuperated as it was by Freud's French re-interpreter Jacques Lacan as "desire for power in our culture"—Freud remarks:

> A third consequence of penis-envy seems to be a loosening of the girl's relation with her mother as a love-object. The situation as a whole is not very clear, but it can be seen that in the end the girl's mother, who sent her into the world so insufficiently equipped, is almost always held responsible for her lack of a penis. The way in which this comes about historically is often that soon after the girl has discovered that her genitals are unsatisfactory she begins to show jealousy of another child on the grounds that her mother is fonder of it than of her, which serves as a reason for her giving up her affectionate relation to her mother. . . .
> . . . Thus the little girl's recognition of the anatomical distinction between the sexes forces her away from masculinity and masculine onanism on to new lines which lead to the development of femininity.
> So far there has been no question of the Oedipus complex, nor has it up to this point played any part. But now the girl's libido slips into a new position by means—there is no other way of putting it—of the equation "penis=child." She gives up her wish for a penis and puts in place of it a wish for a child: and *with this object in view* she takes her father as a love-object. Her mother becomes the object of her jealousy. The girl has turned into a little woman. (pp. 139-140)

socialization: it allows us, forces us, to become social, moral, properly functioning individuals. In so doing, it also outlaws, represses, and rechannels polymorphous pleasure for proper social uses, and as such it is the first and most primal human tragedy, Freud's clinical twentieth-century version of the expulsion from the Garden of Eden.

As Freud consistently argued, civilization was a triumph for the human species and a tragedy for the individual. Freud's own ambivalence about the Oedipus complex hovers over any discussion of such innovative thwartings of it as homosexuality. Freud's account of childhood homosexual development is one part of a strange and unsettling continuum of childhood sexual "disturbances" rather than an exceptional case of pathology. The reason to explore these issues is to make the larger case that the Oedipus complex in Freud's own treatment, despite the urgency of Freud's insistence on its universality, underwent a deeply destabilizing review. Freud often discusses the ways in which the Oedipus complex goes awry for those who emerge as heterosexually oriented, specifically in the case of the masochistic male of the negative Oedipus complex. The masochistic male who emerges as heterosexual doubles the homosexual male in his complex maneuvers to reimagine, innovate, and thwart the normative course of the Oedipus complex. Though a discussion of the negative Oedipus complex exceeds the scope of this essay, the valences that exist between male heterosexual masochism and male homosexual narcissism—both of which processes privilege the *maternal* rather than paternal role in the Oedipus complex—demand a thorough investigation.

Freudian desire: "On narcissism: an introduction"

The erotic predicament that lies at the heart of the Ovidian and Freudian versions of the Narcissus myth is the paradox of desire—the ultimate inaccessibility of another person. Our longing for the other person, our desire to connect to and at times to possess him despite the barriers that separate one person from another, is no less ardent despite their inaccessibility. The Narcissus myth is a heightened, particularly and peculiarly affecting version of the essential pathos of desire—the gulf between self and other. Moreover, thinkers like Freud help us to see that what we long for is our self *in* the other, suggesting, as does Ovid, that desire may not actually proceed from a primary longing for the other but an original desire for self. As Bersani (2001) puts it, all desire, at heart, has a narcissistic basis:

> We love . . . inaccurate versions of ourselves. . . . we relate to difference by recognizing and longing for sameness. All love is, in a sense, homoerotic. Even in the love between a man and a woman, each partner rejoices in finding himself, or herself, in the other. This is not the envy of narcissistic enclosure that Freud thought he detected in male heterosexual desire; it is rather an expression of the security humans can feel when they embrace difference as the supplemental benefit of a universal replication and solidarity of being. Each subject reoccurs differently everywhere. (p. 365)

Given the special emphasis that Freud will place on the homosexual narcissist, and that he begins his discussion with the specific problem of schizophrenia, it is intriguing that Freud frames the entire question of narcissism as a question of a fundamental human need and experience, i.e., love. We "must," Freud (1914) writes, "begin to love in order not to fall ill, and we are bound to fall ill if, in consequence of frustration, we are unable to love." (p. 85). Freud uses narcissism primarily as an opportunity for the discussion of love and a rubric through which to explore it. Here, Freud's controversial penchant for universalization has its most potent, affecting edge as he makes narcissism central to his understanding of human relationships.

Freud (1914) universalizes narcissism within his discussion of the two types of infant's sexual object-choice, which he distinguishes as the anaclitic and the narcissistic. The anaclitic or "attachment" type object-choice focuses on "those persons who are concerned with a child's feeding, care, and protection . . . in the first instance his mother or substitute for her" (p. 87). The narcissistic object-choice can be found "especially clearly in people whose libidinal development has suffered some disturbance, such as perverts and homosexuals, that in their later choice of love-objects they have taken as a model not their mother but their own selves. They are plainly seeking *themselves* as a love-object, and are exhibiting a type of object-choice which must be termed 'narcissistic'" (p. 88). But the next line anticipates Freud's argument that narcissism bears a much greater significance than its prevalence among "perverts and homosexuals" would suggest: "In this observation we have the strongest of the reasons which have led us to adopt the hypothesis of narcissism" (p. 88). Indeed, narcissism's necessity reveals itself in its availability to all individuals as an object-choice. In one of his brilliant turns, Freud reveals narcissism, the special penchant of perverts and homosexuals, as a universal sexual disposition, a primary narcissism that exists in *everyone*:

> We have, however, not concluded that human beings are divided into two sharply differentiated groups, according as their object-choice conforms to the anaclitic or to the narcissistic type; we assume rather that both kinds of object-choice are open to each individual, though he may show a preference for one or the other. We say that a human being has originally two sexual objects—himself and the woman who nurses him—and in doing so we are postulating a primary narcissism in everyone, which may in some cases manifest itself in a dominating fashion in his object-choice. (p. 88)

This universal primary narcissism is complexly significant—and enduringly controversial for psychoanalytic theory. First, it makes it clear that an individual will have not only another person upon whom to fix his erotic hopes, but also himself. Although someone may "show a preference for one or the other," both kinds of object-choice—that involving someone else, that focusing on the self—are available to the desiring subject. I would go further than Freud and say that one can make *both* choices: one can desire oneself as well as someone else. But Freud goes far enough; his language here about the choices open to every individual between anaclitic and narcissistic objects is remarkably neutral even though in the previous paragraph he associates narcissism with those reliable transgressors, perverts and homosexuals. By the time Freud (1914) explains, at a later stage in the essay, that the aim in narcissistic object-choice is to be loved, one has a hard time distinguishing normal from narcissistic—it is the rare person for whom being loved can be of no concern (pp. 100–101).

Freud then proceeds to distinguish anaclitic from narcissistic object-choice in terms that suggest the old, enduring problem of Freud's sexism: males are generally anaclitic in their object relations, females narcissistic. Sexism would appear to be at work here in that the more normative, the anaclitic, model of erotic attraction is generally the domain of males, whereas women and their sexuality are relegated to the sidelines of perversion. Yet because Freud's depiction of narcissism lies suspended between modes of universality and sexual special-ism—just as his view of homosexuality lies between an offhand admiration and a steadfast understanding of it as deviant—the normal heterosexuality of males and the narcissistic perversity of women, while ostensibly the sexual order of things as Freud establishes it, will come to seem less secure and more odd. And, as if presciently aware of our contemporary objections to his limited and limiting views of women, Freud provides one of his most thoughtful demurrals when he qualifies what he's just said about the narcissistic sexuality of women:

> Perhaps it is not out of place here to give an assurance that this description of the feminine form of erotic life *is not due to any tendentious desire on my part to depreciate women.* Apart from the fact that tendentiousness is quite alien to me, I know that these dif-ferent lines of development correspond to the differentiation of functions in a highly complicated biological whole; further, I am ready to admit that there are quite a number of women who love according to the masculine type and who also develop the sexual overvaluation proper to that type. (1914, p. 89, italics added)

And here we have a reminder that what had seemed the nor-mative mode of sexuality, the anaclitic sexuality of men, relies on "overvaluation," a kind of idealizing blindness that makes male desire something less than clear-eyed. Going back to the way that Freud theorized anaclitic male desire, the tendency to overvaluation that characterizes it stems from "*the child's original narcissism and thus corresponds to a transference of that narcissism to the sexual object*" (1914, p. 88, italics added): in other words, at the original heart of the object-choice that provides the nor-mative alternative to perverse narcissism lies narcissism, which engenders the more normative choice. So, narcissism remains the authentic core of any sexual object-choice. I will return to the issue of gendered object-choice below. But for now what I'm seeking to establish is the centrality of narcissism to Freud's thinking about how we desire and how we love. Initially de-scribed as a heretofore unsuspected component of our erotic life, narcissism gathers momentum, emerging as one of the fun-damental principles of desire.

Narcissism even impels the parental love for children. The love parents have for their children revives and reproduces "their own narcissism, which they have long since abandoned" (Frued, 1914 p. 91). Overwhelmed by their potent feelings for their offspring, parents indulge in newly reactivated narcissistic fantasies that they had long suppressed in accordance with "cultural acquisitions" and attempt to extend to their children the narcissistic "privileges which were long ago given up by themselves" (p. 91). If one of the major critiques of Freud's theory of the Oedipus complex is that, in his focus on the oedipal child, he pays insufficient attention to the desires and aggressions of the parents, here, in his theory of narcissism, Freud redresses this oversight, rather frighteningly theorizing parental love for children—commonly perceived as the height of selfless love—as a passionate expression of narcissistic desire: "Parental love, which is so moving and at bottom so childish, is nothing but the parents' narcissism born again" (p. 91). If parental love for children is one of narcissism's masks, it is certainly not the only one. Freud's depiction of narcissism here makes it hard to find a love that is not either a disguised form of narcissism or some kind of attempt to make up for its loss: "A person who loves has, so to speak," Freud states, "forfeited a part of his narcissism, and it can only be replaced by his being loved" (p. 98)—or, as Freud suggests in his depiction of the fond parent, in loving another.

The theme of parental narcissism proves crucial to an understanding of the broad relevance of narcissism to Freud's thinking and also to the depathologizing of homosexual narcissism. It will be helpful to turn to Freud's thinking on heterosexual development and the Oedipus complex—certainly the normative model of human sexual development for Freud—in order to frame our thinking on homosexual narcissism.

the erotic mother: mothers and sons

Jean Laplanche's theory of the "enigmatic signifier" illuminates the questions that attend to the mother-child relationship (Fletcher & Stanton, 1992, pp. 93-120). "Laplanche's concept of the enigmatic signifier," as Bersani (2001) elucidates it,

> refers to an original and unavoidable seduction of the child by the mother, a seduction inherent in the very nurturing of the child. The seduction is not intentional; simply by her care, the parent implants in the child "unconscious and sexual significations" with which the adult world is infiltrated, and that are re-

ceived in the form of an enigmatic signifier—that is, a message by which the child is seduced but that he or she cannot read, an enigmatic message that is perhaps inevitably interpreted as a secret. The result of this original seduction would be a tendency to structure all relations on the basis of an eroticizing mystification. (p. 356)

To take this point further, all sexuality flows from the essentially seductive mother-child relation, in that we always desire enigmatically and that we always desire the enigmatic. As Angelides (2003) further defines Laplanche's concept,

> The enigmatic signifier (of adult desire) is first inscribed in the infant's bodily, or, erotogenic zones. In a second phase, because the child cannot fully or successfully integrate the excessive libidinal excitation, or, unintelligible erotic messages from the parent, this enigmatic signifier undergoes a primal repression. The repressed, residual elements thereafter ensure a permanent conflictual relationship with the ego, producing a subjective core of irreducible otherness. The child is thus split unto him or herself, and sexuality is ever after inflected by an enigmatic otherness. This universal theory of primal seduction and the enigmatic signifier is therefore the foundational structure for the constitution of the primordial unconscious, and thus sexuality, in the child. (p. 93)

As Freud makes remarkably clear, the boundaries separating anaclitic from narcissistic desire are fluid; and as Laplanche suggests, desire begins in the relationship the child has with the mother. Given that the male homosexual's tie to and identification with the mother has been perhaps the most fundamental component of the view of homosexuality as pathological and the theory of male homosexuality itself, it seems well worth considering that desire understood in its *broadest* terms in Freudian thinking stems from the mother-child relationship.

Dean (2001) describes Freud's use of the Narcissus theme in his 1910 essay on Leonardo da Vinci as Freud at his "most inventive" and considers this work part of "a bizarre narrative of Freud's own construction—as if Freud felt compelled to rival Ovid's imaginative genius by creating a story of impossibly elaborate metamorphosis: the transformation of a boy into his mother" (p. 123). "We might say," writes Dean, "that psychoanalysis reveals the otherness within sameness, and so explodes the myth that sameness only involves self-sameness." To take just one example, the boy Leonardo, "by installing his mother in and as his own mind, has become other to himself" (p. 130). This is the radical potential in Freud's treatment that critics such as Michael Warner have overlooked.

Freud called narcissism a wound. If this wound is the customary psychoanalytic lack, lack marks our separation from the powerful being who gave us life alongside our desires—our mothers, whose body we narcissistically mistook for our own. Following Otto Rank, who "argued that the universally traumatic experience of birth is the true origin of all anxiety, not castration," Ian (1993) describes the phallus as the phobic screen for something else: the umbilical cord, which literalizes and symbolizes the trauma of birth and our separation from the mother. Rank did not do away with the central Freudian notion of castration; rather, he theorized that it was birth trauma that alone explained it (p. 21). On some level, all sexuality stems from an essentially traumatic relationship with our mothers and our mothers' bodies. Lacan argued that desire emerges from the differential between need and demand, the moment when our need for the nourishment that comes from the mother's breast transmutes into a demand for the breast not related to the instinctual need for hunger. But we could also argue that desire emanates from the traumatic separation from the body of the woman who gave us life—we want to replace that first fatal cut with the remerging of bodies.

Along these lines, we can interpret narcissism in its manifestation in the homosexual male as a strategy for the repair and restoration of the split, unmoored subject. What the homosexual child (in Freud) desires is to preserve the intensity of the bond between his mother and himself, the feeling of wholeness, of oneness, when he was his mother's own object of desire. Freud doesn't mention, in his treatments of male homosexuality, the concept of parental narcissism, but we do well to remember his discussion of it in "On Narcissism." The mother's own narcissism implicitly drives the process whereby the child learned about desire, how to desire himself, and developed his sustaining fantasy of preserving the scene of maternal desire that was so influential and affecting for the mind and heart and life of the child. The child acutely experiences, one could theorize, the force of the mother's own investment in the child's success in mirroring her own desires, needs for self-reflection, and fantasies of self-perpetuation; the child experiences her own desires, needs, and fantasies so acutely that he begins to imagine that they are *his* desires, needs, and fantasies. Installing his mother's psychic life into his own mind, the child develops a kind of double vision that, on occasion, becomes one: he sees the world both through his mother's eyes and through his own; he seeks to find the same rapturously satisfying image that his mother saw in him; he wishes for the opportunity to see as *she* saw, to find the fulfillment of his own desire reflected in another's face, body, eyes.

One of the problems with the ways in which Freud's theory has been interpreted over the years is that homosexual narcissism's investment in gendered sameness has been taken as an interest in finding oneself replicated, another version of the self. Surely, if Freud has taught us anything, it is that this craving for self-sameness is the *universal* condition of human desire since we all experience the state of primary narcissism. Behind an interest in gendered sameness lies a radical otherness—the mother's desire behind the gazing eyes of the desiring boy, the fantasy that the mother's desire has been incorporated into and enmeshed with one's own.

Because patriarchy insists upon the perpetual reenactment of the Oedipus complex—far from some natural, inherent process, it is the narrative of socialization, the patriarchal script that Freud decoded—the erotic affiliations a male may feel with his mother's desire are never valorized. Given the patriarchal cast of our culture, the only male desire that culture valorizes is that which replicates the desire of the father with whom one has properly identified. Feelings for mothers—the mother's own feelings, a woman's sexual drives and desires, what motivates her own erotic life—have historically been suppressed, repressed, and subordinated. The chief problem the homosexual male has encountered in terms of his desire (and this is to speak of it only within the Freudian context of our discussion) is that it falls precipitously and disastrously outside of the patriarchal, oedipal sphere. Sexism, therefore, accounts just as powerfully and poignantly as homophobia for the pathologization of male homosexuality.

The male homosexual's strategy for preserving the scene of maternal desire resists patriarchal oedipalization, but, as Freud describes it, it is also a different kind of oedipal tragedy; it is a different kind of destruction of the erotic mother-son bond that enables desire even as it demands to be eradicated. Just as the heterosexual male child must abandon the mother as an erotic object, using her as a model for exogamous erotic attraction, the homosexual male must leave behind the mother to proceed with his desiring life. The difference is that the homosexual child devises a brilliant strategy for preserving the mother's role in his desire. This is, of course, only one difference among many.

What drives homosexual desire is what drives *all* desire: an attempt to repair loss, the lack of something we believe we once possessed, somehow, somewhere. If Freud draws upon the terror and violence of the Oedipus myth to describe our first confrontation with adult sexuality, which is to say normative heterosexuality, he draws upon the incomparable frustrations and the plangency of the Narcissus myth to describe homosexuality. Both are tragic myths that mirror each other, providing alternative scenarios of the same theme of impossible desire. They reveal, as does Freud's treatment, that desire is as paradoxically absurd as it is irresistible.

Given that homosexuality has so often been seen as the Oedipus complex gone awry, as a failure to complete the process and be normalized by it, it behooves us to reconsider oedipal conflict. Specifically, it behooves us to reconsider any stable notion of the Oedipus complex in Freud's work, for his views on it are characteristically inconsistent; moreover, the Oedipus complex and its narcissistic-homosexual foil bear far more similarities than are commonly acknowledged. If we can demonstrate the similarities that exist between heterosexual and homosexual development, narcissistic sexuality can be seen as an alternative form of identity to an oedipalized one rather than its stunted inferior. As Lewes (1988) puts it in his superb study *The Psychoanalytic Theory of Male Homosexuality*, "there is no straight line from preoedipal constitution to postoedipal result." Instead, there is only a "bewildering series of transformations." "[T]he mechanisms of the Oedipus complex are really a series of psychic traumas, all results of it are neurotic compromise formations" (p. 82). If it is absurd to see the transition through the Oedipus complex into heterosexuality as a normal, inevitable, natural process, it is also absurd to view narcissistically inclined, mother-identified homosexual childhood development as stunted, counterfeit, unnatural. Though it has been deployed in resolutely homophobic ways throughout American psychiatric history and though it bears the traces of Freud's inconsistent views on homosexuality (certainly far from an exclusively inconsistent Freudian topic), Freud's theory in and of itself seems as plausible a way of theorizing male homosexuality as any other; moreover, it movingly captures the emotional complexity of being a mother-identified male in a patriarchal culture. But perhaps the larger topic here involves what I call Freud's subversive children: children who devise all manner of resisting, thwarting, eluding, and generally mucking up, for distinct reasons, the course of their sexual development, normative or otherwise. The homosexual child is far from the only subversive agent in the Freudian field of childhood sexual development. The masochistic male and the phallic girl join the homosexual child in contesting the consolidation of normative sexual roles into which we must all ostensibly fall.

In the next section, I consider Hawthorne's short story "The Gentle Boy" from a Freudian perspective though not the one influentially limned by Crews (1989). Crews saw the story as a rather unwieldy indulgence on Hawthorne's part in masochistic fantasy (pp. 67-72). What I will suggest is that Freud's theory of male homosexual narcissism here serves as *a general allegory for male sexuality* rather than a minor myth for a sexual minority and as such provides key insights into Hawthorne's story.

gentle boys: Hawthorne and Freud

Nathaniel Hawthorne sets his short story "The Gentle Boy" (written in 1829 and first published the year after) in 1650s Puritan New England.[4] The titular boy, a Quaker named Ilbrahim, is adopted by a Puritan couple, Tobias and Dorothy Pearson, after Tobias discovers the boy mournfully keeping vigil at his father's fresh grave. At this time, the Puritans were actively persecuting the Quakers. Ilbrahim had been in the same jail cell as his imprisoned father and had watched him being hanged. Not

4 All quotes from Hawthorne are taken from the *Centenary Edition* of Hawthorne's works (1962), and page numbers are noted parenthetically in the text.

only have the Puritans killed his father, but they have sentenced his mother to death as well, leaving her to die of exposure in the wilderness. Bereft and abandoned, Ilbrahim occupies a liminal state between life and death. His tenderness and delicacy of spirit are commingled with a "premature manliness," a gravitas born of suffering.

The Quakers match the Puritans' punitive zeal with an ever-increasing proselytizing passion: "The fines, imprisonments, and stripes, liberally distributed by our pious forefathers; the popular antipathy, so strong that it endured nearly a hundred years after actual persecution had ceased, were attractions as powerful for the Quakers, as peace, honor, and reward, would have been for the worldly-minded" (9:69). The strange, delicate, remote child Ilbrahim will be the battleground for contending forces: the sadistic Puritans desiring to squash rebellion and the masochistic Quakers longing for their own persecution. But the most resonant battle rages within Ilbrahim himself, between his desire for his biological mother, the wild, enflamed, visionary Catharine, who evades death in the forest, and for the care and concern of his strong, subdued, steadfast adoptive mother, Dorothy. When the two women meet in a dramatic scene in the church and decide with whom Ilbrahim's fate lies, they form "a practical allegory," "rational piety and unbridled fanaticism, contending for the empire of a young heart" (9:85). Evincing her quiet strength of will throughout the tale, Dorothy unflinchingly withstands the Puritan opprobrium that the Pearsons' adoption of Ilbrahim engenders, whereas her husband Tobias much less steadily stands by his adopted son. Nevertheless, by the tale's close, as Ilbrahim (the boy too gentle for this world) lies dying in his bed, Tobias will embrace the boy's faith.

Let me state the obvious: Hawthorne didn't read Freud and knew nothing of psychoanalysis. When Hawthorne was writing, the term "homosexual" did not exist. Any overlaps between Hawthorne's work and Freud's theory of homosexual childhood development are coincidental, i.e., I have found no evidence that Freud read Hawthorne though it's certainly far from impossible that he did. However, I find remarkable correspondences between Hawthorne's and Freud's depictions of a feminine and female-identified male child. At heart, Freud's theory of male, childhood homosexual development is an account of the process of the development of a male who identifies with the mother rather than the father. Hawthorne allows us to experience the affectional and social ramifications of Freud's theory of this form of male childhood desire. Hawthorne locates in patriarchy a brutally unyielding refusal to tolerate deviance of any kind and a rapacious drive to destroy the most vulnerable and defenseless in its midst. In his delicacy and, most acutely, in his desire to love, Ilbrahim exquisitely embodies Freud's homosexual child, emulating the mother's love for him in his love for another male. In Hawthorne, however, the child emulates a maternal love only haphazardly and incoherently given and attempts to bestow this love on a wholly inadequate and unworthy object. The love Ilbrahim bestows on others is a fantasy enactment of a love he craves but never receives.

Hawthorne uses all of his already considerable skill in this early tale to create in Ilbrahim a figure of strangeness and beauty, qualities that set him apart from the rest of the characters in the story. With his "pale, spiritual face, the eyes that seemed to mingle with the moonlight, the sweet, airy voice, and the outlandish name," Ilbrahim seems more like a visitor from a distant planet than a seventeenth-century New England child: "He was a sweet infant of the skies, that had strayed away from his home" (9:79). By representing Ilbrahim as alien, Hawthorne establishes that a feminine, mother-identified male has no place in this world; Ilbrahim chafes against the masculine, patriarchal Puritan order because the values he embodies can never be affirmed within it. "Quaker" identity in this tale emerges as a broad allegory for phobically perceived differences of all kinds. When Tobias learns that the young, mourning child he attempts to help is Quaker, the "Puritan, who had laid hold of little Ilbrahim's hand, relinquished it as if he were touching a loathsome reptile" (9:73). Difference dissolves human kinship, renders the other a different species altogether.

"Do we not all spring from an evil root?" Tobias then asks himself, allowing his reason to overcome his prejudice. The specificity of this imagery makes a decisive point: Ilbrahim, a queer child, opposes the destructive phallic power of patriarchy. What can be the fate of a "little quiet, lovely boy, whose appearance and deportment were indeed as powerful arguments as could possibly have been adduced in his own favor," in such a grimly oppressive world (9:77)? The stern old man who will turn his "repulsive and unheavenly countenance" against this boy as if he has "polluted" the Puritan church synecdochically stands in for the Puritan community, "a miserable world" toward whom Hawthorne feels a repulsion he can barely contain (9:79).

Dorothy, who immediately takes in the new child as her own, asks Ilbrahim if he has a mother, and "the tears burst forth from his full heart" (9:75). Dorothy tells him to dry his tears "and be my child, as I will be your mother" (9:75). Ilbrahim longs for the oral mother, the original mother with whom he experienced, or wanted to experience, the greatest intimacy; Dorothy represents the oedipal mother, custodian of the social order. While Ilbrahim submits openheartedly to his adoption, it is clear that he never relinquishes his love for Catharine, shown to be almost entirely unsuitable for the role of parent. With her wild, unkempt appearance and feverish, fanatical speeches of condemnation to the Puritans who destroy her and her people, Catharine commands great pity but evokes greater fear. Although Catherine has been abused, victimized, and condemned, her rage and wrath against her oppressors, Hawthorne makes clear, galvanizes as much as it depletes her.

Catharine calls to mind Freud's (1922) indelible portrait of the Medusan mother, who represents the terror of adult sexuality. In the iconography of the Medusa, Freud located a metaphor of castration and the child's attendant revulsion—the writhing snakes being representations of pubic hair and also compensatory substitutions for the castrated penis. If the Medusa's head represents the female genitals—and specifically the "terrifying genitals of the Mother"—it "isolates their horrifying effects from their pleasure-giving ones" (p. 274). Catharine, looming before the Puritans in their church, condemns those who've condemned her: "her raven hair fell down upon her shoulders, and its blackness was defiled by pale streaks of ashes. . . . Her discourse gave evidence of an imagination hopelessly entangled with her reason. . . . She was naturally a woman of mighty passions, and hatred and revenge now wrapped themselves in the garb of piety . . . her denunciations had an almost hellish bitterness" (9:81).

Hawthorne eerily anticipates Freudian themes. He directly pits this Medusan mother against the community that calumniates her and matches her against a different kind of phallic maternity, the coolly rational (though also deeply feeling) oedipal mother Dorothy, who represents the reason and rectitude the community claims to possess but obviously sorely lacks. Indirectly, however, Hawthorne also opposes Medusan Catharine with narcissistically inclined Ilbrahim. Ilbrahim's exquisite tenderness, his feminine disposition, can in no way correspond to the phallic, vengeful fury of the wronged but wrathful Catharine. Nor can Dorothy's courageous and inspiring moral orderliness satisfy Ilbrahim's needs. Ilbrahim roams this inhospitable world in a state of authentic loneliness, in a no man's land of oedipal deprivation. The mother he loves loves her own appropriated phallic power, her rage, above all else, and the mother who loves him loves him from a position within the patriarchal order the boy, in his very essence, opposes. The most positive embodiment of the feminine in the story, the gentle boy provides a stark contrast to the myriad representatives of phallic power—phallic mothers, phallic Puritans, phallically aggressive children—that dominate the tale.

One of Hawthorne's 1837 revisions of the story uncomfortably clarifies *parental* narcissism as one of the major themes of the work.[5] In the original version, when Tobias brings Ilbrahim home for the first time, Dorothy prepares a meal for him that the boy, with tearful tentativeness, manages to eat. But in the revised version of the story, Ilbrahim never eats and Dorothy never makes him a meal. Dorothy and Tobias have lost all of their children; the implication Hawthorne now makes is that the role Ilbrahim serves, that of replacement or substitute for their deceased children, for Dorothy in particular, is more important than his actual, living, breathing, needing person. Even Dorothy, shown to be of far greater courage than her husband and greater benevolence than their community in the revised version, attends to her own needs before those of the child. Ilbrahim's appeasement of her hunger for a child takes the place of the appeasement of his own hunger. Dorothy, therefore, in a far more muted way, resembles Catharine in her ego-absorption. Tobias, shown to be faltering in his resolve to claim Ilbrahim as his own child despite the scorn of his community, seeks

5 For Hawthorne's revisions to "The Gentle Boy," see *The Centenary Edition*, Vol. 9, pp. 613-619.

to repair his own lack of a spiritual life. His primary goal seems to be to find a religious conviction, and so it makes sense that the wild, almost antic, religious zealotry of the Quakers would be seductive to him. In any event, Hawthorne doesn't seem especially interested in Tobias's portions of the narrative. What chiefly interests Hawthorne is the fate of a gentle boy in an ungentle world. I argue that this was Hawthorne's most personal work, and it is for this reason that the themes of the mother-son relationship are central to it.

Hawthorne wrote of his relationship to his own mother that "there has been, ever since my boyhood, a sort of coldness of intercourse between us, such as is apt to come between persons of strong feelings" (8:429). Nevertheless, as Hawthorne's astute recent biographer Brenda Wineapple (2001) writes, the feelings between son and mother "reached deep" (p. 16). Catharine, Ilbrahim's mother, can be seen as a nightmarish version of Elizabeth Manning Hawthorne. Like Catharine, the author's mother had "raven-dark hair," a trait she shared, along with "fine gray eyes," with her son. Both Hawthorne and his mother dreaded separations, several of which they were forced to endure during Hawthorne's fatherless childhood. (Hawthorne's maternal Manning family, who ran a stagecoach business, divided their time between Maine and Massachusetts.) During one separation in 1819, Hawthorne despondently wrote, "I am extremely homesick. Why was I not born a girl that I might have been pinned all my life to my mother's apron?" (15:117).

Mitchell (2000) revises Freud's theory of the Oedipus complex by pointing out that sibling relationships play an equally vital role in childhood development. Along these lines, it is also important to remember that Hawthorne had passionate and complex relationships with his two sisters, Elizabeth and Louisa. "No wonder pairs of women," observes Wineapple (2001), "frequently haunt his fiction. . . . One of the two is usually an exotic beauty, dark-haired, brilliant, and eccentric, like his older sister, Elizabeth; the other, like Marie Louisa, is more overtly conventional, self-effacing, and domestic" (p. 21). In "The Gentle Boy," Catharine can be seen as an Elizabeth figure, Dorothy as a Louisa. Further enhancing the biographical valences of the story, Hawthorne's own father (a sea merchant) died in Surinam when he was very young, and his childhood health was extremely worrisome to his family. And like the unworthy boy that Ilbrahim cares for in the story, the young Hawthorne also suffered in 1813 a foot injury that kept him indoors for several months.

The greatest point of overlap between Hawthorne and his tale lies in Ilbrahim's beauty and the disturbance it creates. Hawthorne came of age in Jacksonian America, a culture that valorized hypermasculine traits and saw effeminacy as a trait associated with degenerate Europe.[6] Hawthorne's own physical beauty, remarked upon by many people throughout his life, was a trait that most likely caused him discomfort in that it made him the object of the gaze.[7] Quoting a biography of Hawthorne by Hawthorne's son-in-law George Lathrop, Henry James (1879) recounts an episode in which Sophia and Elizabeth Peabody,

> desiring to see more of the charming writer, caused him to be invited to a species of conversazione at the house of one of their friends. . . . Several other ladies . . . were as punctual as they, and Hawthorne presently arriving, and seeing a bevy of admirers where he had expected but three or four, fell into a state of agitation, which is vividly described by his biographer. He "stood perfectly motionless, but with a look of a sylvan creature on the point of fleeing away. . . . He was stricken with dismay; his face lost colour and took on a warm paleness . . . his agitation was very great; he stood by a table, and taking up some small object that lay upon it, he found his hand trembling so that he was obliged to lay it down." It was desirable, certainly, that something should occur to break the spell of a diffidence that might justly be called morbid. (p. 54)

This incident graphically portrays Hawthorne's deep discomfort, bordering on frenzy, with being the object of scopophilic

6 See Greven (2005), *Men Beyond Desire, passim,* for a discussion of hypermasculinity in Jacksonian America.

7 My use of the term *gaze* derives from Lacan's reformulation of Freudian theories of scopophilia in Freud's (1905) "Three Essays on the Theory of Sexuality." As Brivic (1991) summarizes it, "[t]he key principle of Lacan's gaze theory is that one can only see something by imagining that it is looking at one." Brivic continues: "One's perceptions, even of landscapes and still lifes, must be motivated by being drawn toward its objects by desire, and desire is always based on an imagined response" (p. 96). It is this imagined response that in vision is called the gaze. Existence itself depends on being gazed at. From the more expansive and specifically feminist use of the term in the work of Mulvey (1975) in her reading of the classic Hollywood cinema, the gaze is exclusively male, a form of looking from a privileged gendered position that renders the woman a sexual spectacle. In Mulveyan terms, Hawthorne was placed in a feminine, passive position against which he apparently chafed: being the object of women's desirous looks.

ardor. James provides another similar anecdote from Lathrop about what would become the famous evening in which the purportedly shy and reclusive Hawthorne sisters brought, at the invitation of Elizabeth Peabody, the New England activist who was the sister of Sophia, who would become Hawthorne's wife, their even shyer and more reclusive brother with them to the Peabody home.

> "Entirely to her surprise," says Mr. Lathrop . . . "entirely to her surprise they came. She herself opened the door, and there, before her, between his sisters, stood a splendidly handsome youth, tall and strong, with no appearance whatever of timidity, but instead an almost fierce determination making his face stern. This was his resource for carrying off the extreme inward tremor which he really felt." (p. 55)

In life, Hawthorne strenuously attempted to overmaster the tremendous anxieties, manifest in trembling hands and inward tremors, the gaze stimulated in him. As Wineapple (2001) writes, Hawthorne's sense of his own masculinity was "unstable"; early on, Hawthorne saw himself as "one apart, marked and wounded, a victim with a special destiny who was, at the same time, as angry as the lame boy in the story 'The Gentle Boy'" (pp. 15 & 31).

Hawthorne makes it quite clear that Ilbrahim's beauty makes his life more difficult. "Even his beauty," the narrator tells us, "and his winning manners, sometimes produced an effect ultimately unfavorable; for the bigots, when the outer surfaces of their iron hearts had been softened and again grew hard, affirmed that no merely natural cause could have so worked upon them" (p. 77). With remarkable insight, Hawthorne describes the difficulties the feminine male encounters in a masculine society. The beauty Ilbrahim possesses, while not a curse, is certainly no gift; unsettling the onlookers, it forces them to punish him, at least in their own minds, for having triggered feelings—of longing or perhaps desire—in them. The male child of beauty encounters the same kinds of phobic treatment suffered by women; he is despised for his witchlike powers to seduce and enthrall through "unnatural" means.

Hawthorne was a male who physically and emotionally resembled his mother and who wrote fiction from a position of "rivalrous identification" with women, as Millicent Bell puts it (1993,

p. 15). Hawthorne, I argue, acutely understands the experience of the narcissistic mother-identified child who wishes to bestow upon someone else the love his mother gave him, or that—here we must add to Freud—he wished that *she* had given *him*. Effeminate, beautiful, tender, and relentlessly persecuted by both other children and their parents, Ilbrahim nevertheless wants nothing more than to bestow his as yet "unappropriated love" on someone else. The someone else who Ilbrahim finds is the reverse of him in every respect. Duplicitous where Ilbrahim is sincere, ugly rather than beautiful, and violently cruel rather than tender, the boy with a leg injury whom Ilbrahim cares for leads Ilbrahim to premature death rather than shared love.

The Pearsons take in and care for this young, male Puritan child who has suffered a leg injury. That his parents are so willing to let another family care for their own child indicates something of this boy's nature. Hawthorne takes pains to let us know that this boy is as physically ugly as he will prove to be spiritually. While this conflation of spiritual with physical character commonly appears in Hawthorne's work and in Victorian literature generally, here it has a deeper significance when considered in light of the story's psychosexual themes.

Ilbrahim, normally adept at decoding physiognomies, fails to read the evil in this boy's physical nature, which the reader, on the other hand, is encouraged to do. He has a disagreeable countenance, slightly distorted mouth, an "irregular, broken" near uni-brow; "an almost imperceptible twist" characterizes his "every joint, and the uneven prominence of the breast." Overall, his body, though "regular in general outline," is "faulty in almost all its details"; moreover, he is "sullen and reserved . . . obtuse in intellect" (9: 90). Nevertheless, Ilbrahim nestles "continually by the bed-side of the little stranger, and, with a fond jealousy" assiduously nurses the boy. Deepening biographical valences, Hawthorne depicts Ilbrahim as a storyteller who recites "imaginary adventures, on the spur of the moment, and in apparently inexhaustible succession," to the convalescent child of "dark and stubborn nature," who responds to Ilbrahim's airy fantasies with remarks of precocious "moral obliquity" (9:91). The force of love emanating from him makes Ilbrahim believe that this love will be returned. One day, seeing the boy he cared for playing with a group of other Puritan children, Ilbrahim approaches them, "as if, having manifested his love to one of them, he had no longer to fear a repulse from their society." But Ilbrahim could not be more mistaken about the lack of reciprocity in matters of love; "the devil of their fathers entered into the unbreeched fanatics," and, shrieking like banshees, they hit Ilbrahim literally with sticks and stones, displaying "an instinct of destruction, far more loathsome than the blood-thirstiness of manhood" (9:92).

The worst part of this brutal assault occurs when the ugly, lame boy whom Ilbrahim has cared for lures Ilbrahim toward him with an offer of protection. Without hesitation, Ilbrahim complies, only to have the "foul-hearted little villain" lift up his staff and strike Ilbrahim on the mouth "so forcibly that blood issued in a stream." Ilbrahim had valiantly attempted to protect himself against this "brood of baby-fiends," but after this brutal version of Judas's kiss, he wholly submits himself to the bashing crowd, an act of supplication that only intensifies their frenzied fury as they "trample upon him" and drag him by his "long, fair locks" (9:92). Some older Puritans happen to rescue him, but Ilbrahim never recovers. Indeed, when Dorothy attempts one day to amuse the utterly withdrawn child, Ilbrahim yields "to a violent display of grief," and during the middle of the night cries "Mother! Mother!" (9:93). Later, on the night that the child Ilbrahim lies dying in his bed, Catharine returns from her world missionary travels and imprisonments, flush with news that Charles II has repealed the hostilities against the Quakers. Ilbrahim dies in her arms, a relief for him and a punishment for Catharine, now wild with grief that she has been "neglectful of the holiest trust which can be committed to a woman" (9:95).

as his mother loved him

Ilbrahim, it would appear, dies of a broken heart, a heart broken by two indistinguishable traitorous loves, that of the boy who returned his love with hate and that of the mother who returned his love with absence. With exquisite economy and pathos, Hawthorne makes vividly clear that Ilbrahim reproduces a fantasy of *being loved* by the mother whom he loves with an equally illusory fantasy of loving and being loved in return by a boy who resembles Ilbrahim, not physically but in his position within Ilbrahim's own fantasy of having been loved and cared for by his mother. Hawthorne enlarges what Freud imagines to be the psychological basis of same-sex desire by representing another dimension of it, that it can also be an enactment of a fantasy for connection between mother and son on the son's part, an expression of longing for maternal love as much as a projection of having been its recipient onto another male. Ilbrahim's grief suggests why narcissism is so directly enmeshed with the grievous heart of all desire, which flows from loss: he mourns for something he has already lost, the mother's love so haphazardly and transitorily given. I don't in any way mean to reduce homosexual desire to a kind of misplaced desire for a mother's love. My chief effort here is to make the case that what Freud theorized as homosexual development retains its validity as one pathway to homosexual orientation. Moreover, it retains its validity as a model of the emotional urgency of mother-identified desire and the difficulties faced by a male who identifies with mother rather than father.

"The Gentle Boy" would appear to be, on the face of it, the height of representations of masochistic male sexuality. Certainly, this is the view of Crews (1989), whose famous (and then famously repudiated by the author himself) Freudian study of Hawthorne theorized that oedipal conflict is the chief psychoanalytic paradigm at work in Hawthorne's writings. Without disputing the importance of masochism to the story, I would argue that it is narcissism, and specifically homosexual narcissism, that informs the tale. If Ilbrahim desires the ugly, lame boy, what he also desires is to reproduce the scene of maternal desire that undergirds his fantasy life; he wants to love this boy *as his mother loved him*, to put it in Freudian terms (1905, p. 145). But, as we have seen, given that it is never clear that Catharine showed Ilbrahim the love he craves and that Catharine has been largely absent from Ilbrahim's brief life, this narcissistic process cannot be said to reproduce Ilbrahim's own childhood experience of maternal desire but to enact a fantasy of its experiential fulfillment.

And herein lies perhaps the deepest poignancy of the tale. Ilbrahim's lavish bestowal of affection on this ugly child—the descriptions of whom border, at first blush, on the gratuitous— reveals a great deal about how he feels about *himself*. If he attempts to make real his mother's desire for him through his desire for and expression of love toward another male, then the fact that the object of his affections is so deeply, clearly, irredeemably unworthy suggests that Ilbrahim sees himself as ugly, base, and unworthy. Further, it shows that he wishes that his mother would have loved him despite these displeasing traits. The disturbing disjuncture between Ilbrahim's actual beauty, readily (if ambivalently) perceived by others, and his fantasy of what he actually is or at least appears to be to himself communicates a great deal about the ways in which social, cultural, and other kinds of experiential messages that convey hatred and revulsion against one's own person affect—indeed shape—one's own image of self. Moreover, Ilbrahim blames himself for his mother's failure to love him or to love him adequately.

The work of Ayers (2003) on the role mother-infant attachment plays in shame provides a deeply resonant insight into Hawthorne's story: "When the maternal intrapsychic conflicts that influence the mother-infant relationship become impingements that in turn become a pattern, the details of the way in which the impingement is sensed by the infant are significant, as well as the infant's reaction to them" (pp. 76–77). The ways in which a child can respond to such emotional abandonment are myriad, and gender and culture will shape the response. Aggression is usually associated with the masculine response, shame with the feminine. I would argue that Ilbrahim clearly reflects the latter response, literally dying of shame—shame at public humiliation and betrayal and shame at his mother's behavior, which he internalizes as behavior he himself caused.

In the end, the enduring value of Hawthorne's and Freud's depictions of the mother-son bond lies in their evocations of the plangency and the urgency of the bond. It would appear that a desire not to perpetuate stereotypes has led modern commentators to eschew if not altogether do away with homosexual narcissism as a way of theorizing gay identity. When contextualized, updated, and freed from pathologizing impetuses, this remains a profound and meaningful way of thinking about some of the varieties of human emotional experience.

references Angelides, S. (2003), Historicizing affect, psychoanalyzing history: pedophilia and the discourse of child sexuality. *Journal of Homosexuality*, 46(1/2):79–109.

Ayers, M. (2003), *Mother-Infant Attachment and Psychoanalysis: The Eyes of Shame*. New York: Brunner-Routledge.

Bayer, R. (1987), *Homosexuality and American Psychiatry: The Politics of Diagnosis*. Princeton, NJ: Princeton University Press.

Bell, M. (1993), Introduction. *New Essays on Hawthorne's Major Tales*. M. Bell, ed. New York: Cambridge University Press.

Bersani, L. (2001), Genital Chastity. *Homosexuality and Psychoanalysis*. T. Dean and C. Lane, eds. Chicago: Chicago University Press.

Brivic, S. (1991), *The Veil of Signs: Joyce, Lacan, and Perception*. Urbana: Illinois University Press.

Crews, F. (1989), *The Sins of the Fathers: Hawthorne's Psychological Themes*. Berkeley: University of California Press.

Dean, T. (2001), Homosexuality and the problem of otherness. *Homosexuality and Psychoanalysis*. T. Dean & C. Lane, eds. Chicago: Chicago University Press.

Dollimore, J. (1991), *Sexual Dissidence: Augustine to Wilde, Freud to Foucault*. New York: Oxford University Press.

Fletcher, J. & M. Stanton, eds. (1992), *Jean Laplanche: Seduction, Translation and the Drives*. London: Institute of Contemporary Arts.

Freud, S. (1905), Three essays on the theory of sexuality. *Standard Edition*. London: Hogarth Press, 7:125–245.

Freud, S. (1914), On narcissism: an introduction. *Standard Edition*. London: Hogarth Press, 14:67–102.

Freud, S. (1922), Medusa's head. *Standard Edition*. London: Hogarth Press, 18:273–274.

Freud, S. (1927), Some psychological consequences of the anatomical distinction between the sexes. *Standard Edition*. London: Hogarth Press, 8:133–142.

Friedman, R. C. & J. I. Downey (2008), *Sexual Orientation and Psychodynamic Psychotherapy: Sexual Science and Clinical Practice*. New York: Columbia University Press.

Fuss, D. (1995), *Identification Papers: Readings on Psychoanalysis, Sexuality and Culture*. New York: Routledge.

Greven, D. (2005), *Men Beyond Desire: Manhood, Sex, and Violation in American Literature.* New York: Palgrave Macmillan.

Hawthorne, N. (1962), *The Centenary Edition of the Works of Nathaniel Hawthorne.* W. Charvat et al., eds. Columbus: Ohio State University Press.

Ian, M. (1993), *Remembering the Phallic Mother: Psychoanalysis, Modernism, and the Fetish.* Ithaca, NY: Cornell University Press.

James, H. (1879), *Hawthorne.* Ithaca, NY: Cornell University Press, 1997.

Lacan, J. (1981), *The Four Fundamental Concepts of Psychoanalysis.* A. Sheridan, trans. New York: Norton.

Lane, C. & T. Dean, eds. (2001), *Homosexuality and Psychoanalysis.* Chicago: Chicago University Press.

Lewes, K. (1988), *The Psychoanalytic Theory of Male Homosexuality.* New York: Simon and Schuster.

Mitchell, J. (2000), *Mad Men and Medusas: Reclaiming Hysteria.* London: The Penguin Press.

Mulvey, L. (1975), Visual pleasure and narrative cinema. *Screen,* 16(3):6–18.

Warner, M. (1990), Homo-narcissism: or, heterosexuality. *Engendering Men: The Question of Male Feminist Criticism.* J. Boone & M. Cadden, eds. New York: Routledge.

Wineapple, B. (2001), Nathaniel Hawthorne 1804-1864: a brief biography. *A Historical Guide to Nathaniel Hawthorne.* L. Reynolds, ed. New York: Oxford University Press.

Dept. of English
Connecticut College
270 Mohegan Ave.
New Haven, CT 06320-4196
dgrev@conncoll.edu

The magic of adoption: a consideration of the preoedipal genesis of the family romance*

Josie Oppenheim

Freud's family romance describes a universal feeling of having been born to parents of exalted status. In this paper the author proposes that the more primal version of this fantasy is that of the magically endowed adopted child. She suggests that the function of this fantasy is to provide a psychical "rapprochement" pathway back to necessary feelings of omnipotence and postulates a universal "adoption experience" from which the fantasy of the magically endowed, adopted child is born.

It is the preoedipal depths of the soul—unfathomable by empathy—into which highly organized man permits only brief glimpses, which appear to be the true "locus" of the magic effect.

Robert Fliess

The magically endowed, adopted child can be considered an archetype, that is, a figure in unconscious fantasy, ubiquitous and materializing in a multitude of cultures and epochs, acquiring costumes and props relevant to the cultural environ of the day. My interest in this paper is to understand what part of our collective experience is contained in this fantasy and how such a familiar protagonist evolved. Further, I am considering whether an illumination of this fantasy can shed some light on how we feel about the real child who has been adopted.

*This paper was originally presented at the National Association for the Advancement of Psychoanalysis's (NAAP's) Continuing Education Committee Seminars, under the title *Psychoanalytic Perspectives on Adoption and Identity: Unconscious Fantasy and the Meanings of Adoption*, at the C. G. Jung Center, May 3, 2008.

The adoptive family has increasingly taken its place within the American mainstream as an accepted minority. Nevertheless, those who have been adopted are subject to feelings of disenfranchisement from a culture where genetic connectedness represents a significant portion of one's identity and self-representation. All minorities evoke feelings of prejudice in others, but as Tolstoy might say, each prejudice is evoked in its own way. While an interest in one's genetic heritage has been shown to be important to an evolving sense of identity for many people, I am suggesting that the concern we feel when a genetic link is absent can function as a screen for repudiated fears and fantasies of a primitive nature leading to an unconscious prejudice against the adopted child. I therefore am seeking to find the ways in which the idea of adoption functions as a symbol both stimulating and suppressing anxiety when we learn of the dual heritage of another.

background

The myths and fairy tales centering around a hero who has been adopted can be understood as precipitates of imagination, as all creative fiction is, and therefore an expression of intrapsychic conflict. But we must also consider that such stories arose from a foundation of actual experience, i.e., from the fact that adoption and other forms of displacement from the home are, and have been, real events, shared by many and visible to many more. For the reality of the stolen child, the displaced child, the adopted child, and the foster child is embedded in world history spanning continents and cultures throughout recorded time (Horner & Rosenberg, 1991).

Dating from antiquity, adoption has held a prominent position in Indian, Mesopotamian, Egyptian, and Roman law (Horner & Rosenberg, 1991). From Roman times to the Renaissance, parents were not required to keep any of the children born to them. "Selling" or "renting" unwanted children was sanctioned by Roman law and also by Hellenistic custom. Parents could also "expose" children in public places, leaving their fate to the "miseria cordedium" or "the kindness of strangers" (Brinich, 1995, pp. 186–187). Records show that China and other Asian communities followed practices similar to those in Europe with regard to displaced children (Horner & Rosenberg, 1991).

During the Dark Ages, unwanted children were often given over to religious communities where they were raised. This practice ended, however, in the twelfth century A.D. when church law decreed that children thus donated were allowed to leave if they so desired when reaching 12 years of age. Thanks to this liberal decree, so many of these children apparently did leave, that monasteries, no longer reaping the benefits of the labor afforded by such children, eventually refused to take them in (Brinich, 1995). With this avenue for unwanted children blocked, parents were "forced to take more drastic measures" (p. 187). Such measures included murder. As Brinich (1995) reports:

> Pope Innocent III (A.D. 1198–1216), appalled by the number of infant bodies he saw floating in the Tiber (Simpson, 1987, p. 136), felt compelled to support the creation of the foundling hospitals which from the thirteenth century onward became the end of the line for many unwanted children. (p. 187)

Though the mortality rate was "abysmal" in these hospitals (Horner & Rosenberg, 1991, p. 140), they represented an enlightened attempt to staunch the more violent solution to unwanted children so many families resorted to (Brinich, 1995).

In more modern times, striking numbers of children are found to have been abandoned in Europe. Records provide evidence of widespread uprooting and displacement through various practices, including fostering and adoption. For example, in the eighteenth century, "about one third of the children born in the diocese of Lyons were abandoned. In . . . Toulouse, one child in every four was known to have been abandoned" (Brinich 1995, p. 187). Perhaps the most startling statistic available reveals that "close to half . . . of all babies baptized in early 19th century Florence were categorized as '*getetello*' (i.e., tossed out)" (p. 187).

The New World, too, figures prominently in the history of the abandoned child with "shiploads of abandoned children taken from the almshouses of major European cities to help populate the American colonies" (Brinich, 1995, p. 187). During the late nineteenth and early twentieth centuries, hundreds of thousands of displaced children were transported on "so-called orphan trains" from eastern American cities to the rural Midwest, where the children were expected to work (p. 187).

The history of adoption and dual heritage allows us to see that the child's security in her family is far from guaranteed (Horner & Rosenberg, 1991). Adults, often in circumstances that reduce their options or even render them helpless, nevertheless are usually all powerful with respect to their children, able to abandon them, place them in the care of the state, or seek out alternate homes where they will be better provided for. As Brinich (1995) states:

> [D]ata . . . drawn from Roman times, the Middle Ages, the Renaissance, colonial America, and the past century of American history . . . reveal that, throughout recorded history, some parents have always abandoned some of their children . . . [whether] motivated by immediate economic necessity; . . . shame; or deeper, intrapsychic conflicts. (p. 187)[1]

Yet, as Brinich (1995) points out, parental seductions, battered child syndrome, and other forms of child abuse are indications that "abandonment," no matter what the cause, "is often a relatively benign outcome of parental ambivalence" (p. 187).

We can assume that children are sensitive to the breach in security parental ambivalence might represent. Block (1974), in her article "Fantasy and the Fear of Infanticide" and elsewhere has shown that children are very aware of their vulnerability with respect to parental ambivalence and create all sorts of fantasies to shield themselves from the fear of being killed by their parents. Sensitive to the murderous feelings that all parents experience to a greater or lesser degree, children believe that their own annihilation at the hands of large, powerful beings who demonstrate rageful feelings or even negative emotions is possible. Block places the genesis of the child's ubiquitous fear of monsters and other imaginary threats squarely with the parents, overlarge beings who can rightly be perceived as dangerous. How much easier is it, then, for a child to consider abandonment a reality, at least unconsciously. One can assume that the fear of abandonment is hardwired to insure survival. Liedloff

---

1 Though historians often refer to adoption as a form of abandonment, the attempt to provide a more viable life for one's child than would be possible otherwise is not, in fact, abandonment, but a series of pragmatic, psychological and legal steps set into motion to secure the child's adoptive family.

(1986) describes how children in tribal cultures, not penned in by the bars of a playground, never have to be coaxed to leave; the adult group simply moves on according to its needs, and the children immediately run after, instinctively knowing their survival depends on proximity to adults.

An example of this fear of abandonment was given me by a patient, Ms. R, the mother of a six-year-old child. Embarking upon a trial separation from her husband, Ms. R had set aside an evening to begin talking to her child about the change. The child, upon hearing that her parents were going to be "living separately," immediately began to sob and seemed inconsolable. Ms. R was distraught, thinking her daughter would not be able to weather such a disruption. However, upon questioning, it emerged that the child's concerns were elsewhere. "Who's going to take care of me?" she asked, convinced that her parents had decided to leave her alone in the apartment while they each found separate places to live away from her. When Ms. R explained that mother and daughter would remain together in their current home with regular visits from the father, the crying immediately stopped.

Because the separation of the parents did not pose an immediate threat to the child's survival, she was actually relieved to find it was only one parent who would be moving, and her mother would be there taking care of her at all times. While we can conjecture that there were many reasons for this child to have heightened fears of abandonment, her reaction, nevertheless, shows how close to the surface can be the genuine belief in the possibility of imminent abandonment and dislocation in a child although such fears may be well disguised and concealed from view.

The displaced child, then, is a fact of human existence, and the potential for displacement is likely processed by all children, those who have been adopted and those who have not, in different ways, according to age, circumstance and level of development (Horner & Rosenberg, 1991; A. Freud, 1968). The intrapsychic defenses against such knowledge may take many forms and may be partially gleaned in the stories of lost, stolen, and adopted children in folklore and myth. These historical artifacts are also psychical artifacts and continue to hold our interest, leading as they may, like Hansel and Gretel's shiny pebbles and disappearing bread crumbs, to the sociocultural reality of an earlier time, but also to our own barely visible, archaic experience.

the magical adopted child

The stories of adopted heroes, adopted animals, changelings, and magically endowed adopted children are ubiquitous in myth, comic books, fairy tales, children's literature, the Bible. In short this theme is so prevalent in so many forms and in so many cultures, it would seem to reflect a universal fantasy, indicating a structural aspect of the psyche. A small sampling of these adopted protagonists who are often magically endowed include Oedipus, Moses, Hercules, Peter Pan, The Ugly Duckling, Superman, various heroes in the Indian epic *The Mahabharata*, and Babar. If one allows, as a reflection of the same fantasy, a dual heritage with one magical parent and another ordinary one, we can include Jesus, Cinderella, Achilles, Aeneas, and many others.[2] Sometimes the situation is reversed: the original parents are human and the adoptive parent—usually an abductor—is magical. Here we can include Rapunzel, Hansel and Gretel, and Dorothy of *The Wizard of Oz*.[3]

The most current example of an adopted hero with magical origins is Harry Potter, a character in literature who appears to be a myth in the making. Harry's adoptive parents force him to live in a closet and subject him to humiliation and deprivation while

2 One can interpret that these stories, where one parent is magical and the other ordinary, corresponds to a later stage in development. As Freud (1909) delineates, the older child learns that paternity is never really certain while maternity can be assured. The fantasy of having been adopted is modified so that the father alone is exalted, whereas the mother remains as she is in reality. Here, as mentioned, the Christian narrative of a child born of an ordinary woman and fathered by God is a good example.

3 This last presents a dizzying array of adoptions and re-adoptions for the latency-aged heroine. Dorothy is adopted by an aunt and uncle, then by a good witch, a bad witch (magical parents), and finally a magical wizard. The wizard is depicted in the film as nothing but a huge face hovering above, a prototype of an image I discuss later. The wizard becomes all too human, unveiled by the knowledge conferred by Dorothy's development. He is nevertheless able to help her, in part because of his easy familiarity with primary process and magical thinking, e.g., the Scarecrow's diploma equals a brain. Dorothy's developmental journey requires a revisiting of the more purely subjective, magical realm in order, it would seem, to fortify her for the tasks of impending adolescence and adulthood in a life that is perhaps too starkly devoid of her omnipotence. (See later discussion of omnipotence under *Some Meanings and Uses of Magic* and *Unconscious Fantasy, Hallucinations, and Magic*.)

they overindulge the exceedingly obnoxious child born to them. Harry, a boy Cinderella, escapes to the ball—Hogwarts, a school for wizards—with the help of his version of a fairy godmother, a magnificent giant of a wizard who mercifully, to the reader, frightens and humiliates Harry's cruel, adoptive family. At Hogwarts, Harry finds friends and mentors and a much more suitable adoptive family. His biological parents, he discovers, were both wizards, and he too is a wizard able, now, to partake of his birthright. Magic is his realm, and he wields the power of magic.

A patient, Ms. B, described her concern when Danielle, her 12-year-old daughter, became increasingly obsessed with the Harry Potter stories. Danielle watched the films over and over on her computer, plastered the walls of her room with scenes from the movies, wore a wizard's cape to school, and wielded a wand as she repeated incantations, curses, and spells throughout the day. She often appeared to be lost in the world of Hogwarts, the ancient school for wizards and witches, seeming to shun contact with her classmates in favor of the imaginary, magical band of friends.

We understood Danielle's obsession to be connected to the fact that my patient had adopted her daughter in infancy. This fantasy seemed to provide a way to put off the daunting tasks of adolescence and supplied a resolution to the phase-appropriate confusion of identity made more complex by the fact of Danielle's dual heritage.

I am suggesting, however, that the theme of adoption in literature has a universal significance that goes beyond an appeal to those who have been personally affected by the fact of adoption and that the latent meanings of the stories and myths on this subject reside in us as well as in the myths. The fascination with Harry Potter is certainly not limited to children who have been adopted, just as Superman was not. Testament to that fact is the fairy tale rags-to-riches rise of J. K. Rowling, who escaped a life on the dole and has become one of the wealthiest people alive, thanks to the epic tale within her of an adopted hero with magical beginnings.

But what is the meaning of this adopted hero? What universal experience of human development is it describing? For though it is true that the real history of dislocated and abandoned children may give rise to the many myths and tales of adopted and step-parented children (Horner & Rosenberg, 1991), we can assume that the presence of magic indicates a meaningful intrapsychic experience that is unconsciously understood within a context protected from the reality principle.

some meanings and uses of magic

Magic has many meanings, but its general use refers to the invoking of supernatural forces to manipulate the physical world according to one's will (Freud, 1913). In infancy, if nothing goes too wrong, it is the mother or maternal figure who functions as a being imbued with magic. According to Winnicott (1953), it is the mother's job to function not only as a caretaker, but as one who manages reality so that it aligns with the infant's magical thinking. It is easy to see that the idea of God or gods residing above us describes the earliest experience of the mother or primary caretaker. From the infant's point of view, the face of the mother hovers above, bends beneficently toward the infant to bring it to her all-encompassing self, becomes a magical, healing, and revitalizing substance, and conveys a seemingly infinite certitude of safety and peace. If all goes well, it is the infant's need and wish for the magical or supernatural being that often enough brings her forth (Winnicott, 1953) and so, like Chanticleer the rooster who believed his crowing caused the sun to rise, the infant, too, experiences itself as magically endowed, at least sometimes.

Though we are accustomed to thinking of the breast as the locus of the infant's interest, Spitz (1983), in an impassioned plea for observation, exhorts us to understand that the infant does not configure the breast as its primary part-object:

> The nursing baby does not look at the *breast*. He does not look at the breast when the mother is approaching him, nor when she is offering him the breast, nor when he is nursing. He stares unwaveringly, from the beginning of the feeding to the end of it, at the mother's face . . . the infant, while nursing at the breast, is at the same time staring at the mother's face; thus breast and face are experienced as one and indivisible. (p. 218)

Utilizing psychoanalytic material reported to Lewin and others, Spitz (1983) deduces that the nipple in the mouth, the feel of the mother's skin, the grasping hand of the infant, and the face and eyes of the mother form, all at once, the nursing experience for the infant with its component parts not separable from the gestalt. Spitz also insists that it is not hunger that impinges on the infant, but thirst and dryness that cause the distress. These common sense observations have some bearing on my understanding of magical fantasy and the symbols that have evolved to contain it. It is why, for instance, that I say the hovering face becomes, for the infant, the supernatural being itself, and why we say we are "drinking in" the sight of something or someone who is giving pleasure or bringing something needed. For the infant, the mother's face *is* the revitalizing substance, the milk that in actuality, of course, emanates from the breast.

As the reality of cause and effect begins to hold sway for the developing child, the magic of the supernatural beings is abandoned, or at least relegated to the unconscious. For the child begins to walk on her own and can point to an object she wants and can even vociferously say, "No." Society, however, makes certain, through the agency of the parent, that developmental progress will not include an abandonment of magic for it is imposed once again upon the individuating child almost by force. The fact is the very young child whose task it is to differentiate the subjective from the objective is hindered in this endeavor. For as the child is learning to navigate the world with her own developing powers and gaining a greater understanding of "me" and "not me," magic is reintroduced in symbolic form as God. The cultural shift from religion to a belief in science has not done away with the magical protection of a god, a saint, or the luck-giving Ganesha. Families who do not identify with a religious belief in God or gods (along with families who do), nevertheless, supply for their children loosely organized ceremonies and rituals in support of secular traditions involving magic, such as Santa Claus and the Tooth Fairy. Fairy tales are introduced at this time as well as other magical ideas. Why the human social group offers magic up to its developing young is a complex question and outside the scope of this investigation, but it would seem that a belief in some magic some of the time is beneficial to the child and/or to the group. If magic is understood as pertaining to the early experience of omnipotence, then some understanding of its continuing necessity becomes possible.

Winnicott (1945) suggests, in a precursor to his theory of the transitional object, that the infant must be made to believe that the hallucinated breast and the real breast are one and the same although they are not. This idea resonates, I believe, with our actual experience of subjectivity and with our understanding of the ever-present transferences in analysis and in life. The inner idea and reality overlap with the subjective providing the only means of approaching the outer, but also obscuring and confusing it. Too much reality, however, too great a loss of the normally overlapping and enveloping magical belief in our omnipotence would constitute a narcissistic blow likely to devastate our abilities to navigate through the subjective to the objective and back again. We can conjecture that a psychosis may erupt like a fever as a means to reinstate the sense of omnipotence when the objective world overwhelms.

unconscious fantasy, hallucinations, and magic

Freud (1900) believed that dreams are hallucinations that occur in sleep, whereas waking hallucinations are resorted to in psychotic functioning. Hallucinations are not, however, relegated only to sleep and psychotic states. Hallucinated sensation is an adaptive capability that apparently is ubiquitous. For example, hallucinated sensation brings about physiological responses such as secretions, sneezing, and sexual tumescence (Dorpat, 1968). Studies have shown that the sensation of a stimulus is often achieved through a pathway to memory traces of an earlier stimulus and that only when the remembered sensation is activated is a physiological response triggered. It is taste, in other words, and the hallucinated memory of earlier taste that triggers salivation, not the food itself. Negative hallucinations, i.e., anesthetic states brought about by conversion symptoms or hypnotic suggestion, stop sensation that would normally occur from an external stimulus. In other words, when sensation is anesthetized, the expected physiological response does not occur. For example, when an irritant was injected under the skin in a group hypnotically directed to have no feeling, a rash did not appear, while the expected rash did appear in those who were not hypnotically anesthetized. This fact implies that sensations (and not the external stimulus) bring about important physiological responses. Dorpat proposes that "the central nervous system control of certain somatic actions is mediated by *psychological* processes that regulate the formation of sensations (p. 319, italics added).

One could conjecture, then, that feelings of the magical or thoughts of magic provide a pathway to the memory of the hallucinated, omnipotent self that in turn provides an emotional feeding triggering physiological and affective responses that are fortifying and beneficial to the psyche and the soma. Magical belief, thoughts, or feelings would be, then, the psychical analog of Mahler's (Mahler, Pine & Bergman, 1975) rapprochement phase, a necessary return to the hallucinatory memory of the magical omnipotence conferred by the mother in order to refuel for greater integration and individuation. Such refueling would become especially important when development or trauma threaten to erode the already established narcissistic foundation.

Human beings are naturally afforded many opportunities for sensations that are felt as magical and have created many more avenues for receiving this enlivened feeling, this thrill of the magical possibility. A good poker hand, for example, confers such a feeling, a sudden belief that one's very wish has brought forth these exciting and powerful cards. A mere self-activated attitude of concentration or prayer, it seems, will miraculously provide the player with the next sought-after card. Good cards are proof of the player's right to dwell in a world where pleasure, power, and magical sustenance, imbibed by visually "drinking in" the beautiful cards, coalesce. A bad draw relegates the player to helplessness and despair, a world of haphazard numbers and chaotic patterns—a club and a spade here, a six and a three there—wherein meaning cannot be construed, and one is shut out of the magical sphere, left to fend for oneself in the heartless world of accident. The highs and lows of poker can be seen to replicate the infant's feeling states. The failure of the mother's face to appear in response to the baby's wish creates a heartless world without meaning. Her appearance provides enlivening power and sustenance from a magical pool of resources. Cards, it may be interesting to note, are said to have faces.

Artists are magicians par excellence and are well known to suffer tremendous depressions that alternate with soaring states of ecstasy. These shifts in feeling states are often directly related to the vicissitudes of their work. If we consider that aesthetic acumen amounts to an obsession with subtle harmonies, a rigorous concern with structural demands, a scientific investigation into what "works" and a continuous desire to understand the essence of beauty, we might find it is plausible that the artist's now unconscious and sublimated wish is to reconstruct the mother's face and to find it magically appearing before the artist at will. Black despair and rage may descend should the artist misstep and not find, in the moment, the aesthetic means to achieve the vision that represents the return of the mother's face, or the restructuring of the mother's expression so that she is no longer Green's (2001) dead mother but the mother engaged in Bion's reverie. Cezanne's concentration in this magical act was so acute that the sound of a dog barking far in the distance caused him to pack up his easel and return home. On the many occasions he felt unable to wield the power of his magic, the wand/brush, no longer responsive to his incantations, became an ordinary instrument of destruction as he mercilessly stabbed holes in the offending canvas, often to the horror of those who felt the painting was one more product of Cezanne's prodigious genius (Perruchot, 1958).

Cezanne suggested that the artist approach a portrait as if it were a landscape: a brilliant way to lose the conceptual connection to the "faceness" of a face. A face was to be abstracted to its component parts so that the human meaning was temporarily obscured. Each plane and tone was to be coolly assessed and established until the humanness could blend properly with the laws of physics, allowing a truer, more correct reconstruction to be revealed. Interestingly, sensation was Cezanne's proclaimed master, aiding and directing the impressions set down (Perruchot, 1958; Rewald, 1968). If we employ Freud's (1900) mechanism of reversal in psychic life, we can infer that a landscape was, concomitantly, to be approached as a face, at least in the sense I have suggested. That is, the excitement and beauty of the landscape was to be created through the artist's magical powers as the face of the mother was magically evoked by the wish of the infant.

Freud (1913) would perhaps not disagree, entirely, with this idea of art:

People speak with justice of the "magic of art" and compare artists to magicians. But the comparison is perhaps more significant than it claims to be. There can be no doubt that art did not begin as art for art's sake. It worked originally in the service of impulses which are for the most part extinct to-day. And among them we may suspect the presence of many magical purposes. (p. 90)

And in a footnote, Freud says:

In Reinach's opinion the primitive artists who left behind the carvings and paintings of animals in the French caves, did not desire to "please" but to "evoke" or conjure up. He thus explains why it is that these pictures are situated in the darkest and most inaccessible parts of the caves and that dangerous beasts of prey do not appear among them. (pp. 90–91, fn. 3)

Even the "dark arts," to use a Harry Potter term, can reinstate a necessary belief in the sustaining omnipotence of oneself or of another. A patient described waking up in the middle of the night as a young child and calling out for her parents who, mysteriously, did not respond. She cried out louder and louder, but still no one came. Though she was old enough to get up and rouse her parents, she felt rooted to the bed. Helpless and alone, she became convinced that a witch had cast a spell on her sleeping parents and that they could not hear her. She continued to cry for a long time and to call out for them until finally she fell asleep. In the morning everything had returned to normal, her parents were there, she had breakfast, and she went to school. She never brought up this terrifying experience to her parents, but as an adult she mentioned it to her mother, who responded that they must have been at a neighbor's house and that they always visited that neighbor at night while their child slept.

In the early part of treatment this patient described many hallucinations she had had as a child. In the analysis, over time, she came to understand that the belief in the witch, as frightening as it was, had probably been resorted to as a protection. For had she actually found herself alone in the darkened apartment with no understanding of where her parents might be, with no number to call if she needed help, with no one to suggest the parents would ever return, her fear would have been intolerable. The witch allowed her to remain magically paralyzed and to cry herself to sleep and provided, in fact, a protective presence that shielded her from a reality she could not have managed. The witch, then, was the absent mother, experienced as a present bad mother, who nevertheless shielded her—as a good mother would—from the fragmenting lack of meaning that would intrude should the human connection be severed.

As we are all gamblers some of the time, and geniuses more often, magical feelings abound and can be triggered by an outside occurrence, or they can be hallucinated or imagined or simply "felt." Usually they involve an accident of circumstance that overlaps an inner need to restructure the mother's face— to reinstate one's omnipotence in relation to a feeling of loss.

Freud's (1907) anecdote of an otherwise rational man who succumbed to a feeling of the supernatural provides an example of how circumstance and inner wish coincide in a magical moment:

> I know of a doctor who had once lost one of his women patients suffering from Graves' disease, and who could not get rid of a faint suspicion that he might perhaps have contributed to the unhappy outcome by a thoughtless prescription. One day, several years later, a girl entered his consulting-room, who, in spite of all his efforts, he could not help recognizing as the dead one. He could frame only a single thought: "So after all it's true that the dead can come back to life." His dread did not give way to shame till the girl introduced herself as the sister of the one who had died of the same disease as she herself was suffering from. The victims of Graves' disease, as has often been observed, have a marked facial resemblance to one another; and in this case this typical likeness was reinforced by a family one. The doctor to whom this occurred was, however, none other than myself. (pp. 71–72)

But this was no idle mistake; the trauma of the death of Freud's baby brother, when Freud was two and a half, no doubt was revisited by the unexpected sight of a surviving, but perhaps soon to die, sibling with whom Freud probably identified as a surviving sibling. And so Freud's wish that his dead brother could magically reappear, establishing the possibility that Freud himself might evade death, was granted with the hallucination or illusion of a revenant, a dead girl, living again and the resultant thought that the "dead can return."

Much of Freud's character was formed by his brother's death and the fear of his own death or sudden disappearance that it engendered (Schur, 1972). Evidence of this is perhaps strongest in his characteristic parting remark of "Goodbye, you may never see me again" (Schur, 1972; Jones, 1957). So the need to restore the feeling of omnipotence was probably acute upon seeing the dying sibling of a patient whose death Freud partially blamed on himself. By bringing the dead patient to life, Freud was, metaphorically speaking, reconstructing the mother's face in order to restore a primeval, magical realm to protect him from the terrifying thought of severance from the archaic mother in the permanent disappearance wrought by death.

why the magical hero is adopted

These thoughts about the importance of magical experience as a protection, repair, and support for the primacy of healthy narcissism leave unaddressed the question of why magical heroes and heroines are so often adopted. It is my hypothesis that the omnipresence of the magically endowed adopted child in myth and literature exists because the feeling of being not quite properly connected to one's parents is common to us all. This universal feeling gives rise to a fantasy, sometimes conscious and sometimes not, of having been adopted by one's present parents, with a shadowy presentiment of another set of parents, thought to be obscured by the amnesia of childhood. In fact the parents remain, in most cases, the biological parents one was born to. In all cases, I believe, for adopted children and for those who are not adopted, it is the magical dyadic era that is not remembered, yet mourned. Of course actual separation, leading to an adoption or simply loss, complicates this universal mourning.

P. L. Travers, the author of *Mary Poppins*, another English tale involving an adoption, wrote about this era and linked its loss persuasively and poignantly to the acquisition of language. In a chapter entitled "John and Barbara's Story," Mary Poppins is in the nursery folding laundry and watching the Banks's baby twins, John and Barbara, who should be napping but are babbling in their cribs. They are too little to speak, but they can "magically" communicate with a patch of sunlight and also with an irascible sparrow that often comes to visit. And they can also speak to Mary Poppins, whom the sparrow says is the only adult who has retained this magic language, a language we would understand as preverbal. Mary Poppins and the sparrow explain to the children that when they are a little older, they will lose their ability to chat with the wind and the stars and everything else. The twins are devastated that they will be as limited as the adults and refuse to believe it, wailing at the thought. The sparrow flies off and returns after a few months' vacation to find that the twins no longer understand what he is saying. He looks at Mary Poppins—a stern and stingingly sarcastic character (she is a much more severe, odd, and matronly character in Travers's rendering of her than she is in the film)—and she barely nods in assent of his realization; yes, the twins have learned to speak. And yes, of course, they no longer understand the sparrow. The sparrow, also stingingly sarcastic and unsentimental, hides his tears, embarrassing evidence of his affection for the twins and of his and their loss; it is the bittersweet loss that comes with development, the pain of which is so keenly felt with this story that one can only tolerate it, one feels, because of the continuing presence of the fierce, uncompromising, no-nonsense, yet, paradoxically, magical nanny. Her ability to continuously push her charges forward while providing a magical world of their dreams could be seen as a prototype for the psychoanalytic endeavor with the analyst providing a relationship to move the child/patient back in time toward omnipotence and forward into his rightful place in the social realm.

Freud (1909) wrote in "Family Romances" that the fantasy of having been adopted was a solution to the oedipal dilemma, while also allowing the child to retain the idealized qualities of the parents that greater cognition calls into question. I am attempting to bring into relief the more primal component to this fantasy that I believe is the precursor and the foundation for Freud's oedipal phase fantasy. This component has evolved out of the infinite, subtle, and not so subtle, experiences of what might be imagined as the systolic and diastolic rhythm of merger and separation in early life. These pulses of merger alternating with separateness provide the experiential material for the fantasy of two sets of parents as it is understood and elaborated in later development.[4]

As the child grows, life presents even more opportunities for extended separations from the dyadic union. Some of these separations are pleasurable, some are optimal for growth, and some are traumatic (Kohut, 1968). I am proposing that each of these separations, no matter what the emotional valence, can be under-

4 This idea is of course related to Klein's (1946) splitting mechanisms that occur during the primitive era of the paranoid schizoid position.

stood as "an adoption experience," for in each such experience the child has been placed, if only briefly, in the care of an entity that is not the primary caregiver. I use the term "entity" because the child will, one can assume, experience the environment as the caretaker when an actual caretaker is absent, just as the lack of the breast (understood here to refer to the breast/face of the nursing gestalt) is, in the beginning, experienced by the child not as an absence, but as an existing bad breast (Klein, 1946; Bion, 1962). When a child is taken from the mother at birth and thrust into a nursery with other newborns, the environment of the nursery has adopted the child. Another example of how the absence of human contact is felt as a present "bad" surrogate or adoptive mother can be seen in my patient who found herself alone at night. The room itself became the witch, represented by, as she put it, "darkness permeated with yellow and white circles of light."

Over time, there are more and more separations from the maternal environment—a doctor, a camp counselor, a new pal, or special crowd—each provides an "adoption experience." The employment of wet nurses was certainly a practice that amounted to a form of adoption for the mother, child, and wet nurse. One might say that what Freud termed transference occurs in instances where there is a transference of care from an internalized and projected maternal environment to a new, actual environment, for such transferences occur when one feels the hope or fear that the object of the transference will become a caretaker or "adoptive" parent. The behaviors activated with respect to a transferential object are, in a sense, strivings and defenses employed by all of us "adoptees" in an attempt to make the adoption work, whether the transference-object be an employer, a friend, or the analyst.

the real adopted child

My interest in the magically endowed adopted child as a protagonist in an unconscious fantasy that has a universal genesis and appeal stems from my interest in how adoption is experienced by those who do not have a familial connection to it. This interest grew out of my work with patients in adoptive families who reported comments, sometimes well meaning, from strangers, friends, and family that revealed an uneasy, not quite accepting attitude with respect to someone whose origins included a dual heritage. Most adoptive families have been subjected to comments that indicate that a child who has been adopted is inherently "different" or that the parent/child bond is inadequate. Adoptive families report being exposed to comments that trigger feelings of being less real, less belonging to each other, less legitimately connected to each other.

A patient, Mr. H, the assistant principal of a progressive private school, reported that in a meeting to discuss recent family interviews with prospective students, the principal had said, "All adopted kids are weird!" The comment was used in support of the school's not accepting a child who had been adopted, despite two excellent interviews and good reports from his preschool. Mr. H himself had been adopted, but had chosen not to disclose that fact as a protection against what he experienced as a subtle, "shut down" response in those he told.

Another patient, Mr. L, the adoptive father of a nine-year-old boy, reported that he had gone to the home of his niece, a young woman who was pregnant and had been told she was having a boy. Several family members and friends were present. Wandering into the dining room to get something to drink, Mr. L overheard his mother-in-law speaking to several friends about the niece's pregnancy. Apparently unaware of Mr. L's presence his mother-in-law said joyously, "I'm so glad we're finally going to have a boy in the family!" This woman was the grandmother of five girls, so the comment was very understandable except for the fact that she was also the grandmother of Mr. L's son who had been adopted at four months and who had had the distinction in the family of being the only boy of the six grandchildren for close to nine years. What made this comment particularly painful, Mr. L told me, was that his mother-in-law had always been an important presence for his son and for him, helping financially and in general being a support and an ally.

In both these reports a bias against the adopted child becomes evident. In the first, the bias is conscious and expressed directly. In the second, the bias is, very likely, unconscious.

A third example was reported by Mrs. S. In a meeting with her seven-year-old daughter's teacher, Mrs. S was discussing various concerns about her daughter's academic performance. Shifting to her child's strengths, she mentioned that her daughter had an incredible sensitivity to music. The teacher responded, saying, "Her parents must have been musical." At first Mrs. S was confused (neither she nor her husband had a particular connection to music) and then greatly shocked to realize that the teacher was referring to the child's biological parents without speaking in any way that would acknowledge that Mrs. S was the child's parent. This patient, having adopted her daughter at seven months, described to me how, in one instant, all the joys and trials of parenthood, the sleepless nights, the potty training, the thrill of her daughter's first words, the terror she had experienced when there was concern about a serious illness, the agony when the child actually contracted a serious condition, her confusion over how to appropriately set limits, her pride in her daughter's many talents—all this seemed to vanish as she saw herself in the teacher's eyes as someone who did not belong to her child and whose child did not belong to her.

Adoptive families—children and parents—usually cannot help overhearing comments on television or by strangers or within their extended families that trigger feelings of being cast out. Comments from strangers that the child has been saved by the adoptive parent, while well meaning, indicate that children who have been adopted are often seen not as a blessing to their parents, as other children are, but as blessed for being rescued. This desire to see the adopted child as rescued may, however, in some cases, represent a desire on the commenter's part to be rescued from her own anxieties about abandonment.

The unconscious fantasy that we have been separated from our magical parents and adopted by muggles—Rowling's term for ordinary people who are outside the magical realm—can contrast sharply with the feelings aroused by a living child or adult who has been adopted. For the real adopted child has, in most cases, been permanently severed from what is believed, in our unconscious, to be a magical realm. The magical child in myth and story, who has been adopted into a non-magical realm is allowed, in fact often required, to return to the magical realm in a rapprochement maneuver that stimulates in us, when we read about it, sensations of remembered omnipotence. But the real adopted child may symbolize our inability to return, our inability to be magically lifted and magically nourished. The real adopted child threatens to activate sensations of deflation, helplessness, and lack of meaning. This is why feelings aroused by the adopted child are often instantly repudiated, while the magical, adopted hero or heroine, who stimulates sensations of regained omnipotence, is romanticized, idealized, joined, internalized. This regaining of a sensation of omnipotence may be the reason that inmates in Guantanamo Prison choose, above all other possibilities, the Harry Potter books.[5]

Stories and myths are created to contain our experiences and mirror them back to us: the story of birth is the story of connectedness and belonging while the story of adoption is the story of separation. But a symbol may contain its opposite as well. The story of pregnancy and birth is also the story of an alien being invading the body and causing destruction, and the story of adoption is also the story of inclusion and the relief from the pressures of acquiring a baby through physical pain and dangerous sexual encounters.

A 15-year-old girl, a patient who had been adopted as an infant, described how she did not like her boyfriend's saying it was sexy that they talked on the phone for so long. In exploring why she did not like this, I suggested that it might be sexy because it implied that they were close. The girl was resistant to this idea, so I suggested that perhaps closeness might lead to . . . ? Here I was vague and indicated that she should fill in the blank, but I was thinking of cuddling or kissing or some physical contact. I knew that the patient was phobic about even speaking of such things. The girl circumvented my lead and said, "love." "Yes," I agreed, "closeness leads to love; and love leads to . . . ?" Again, the girl cleverly sidestepped and replied, "marriage." Of course I had to agree once again, so I said "Yes, and marriage leads to . . . ?" I was still looking for some acknowledgement that sex exists, at least in married life. This time the girl jumped in eagerly and with great apparent pleasure exclaimed, "Adoption!"

This young patient obviously derived pleasure from cleverly foiling my attempts to get her to acknowledge sex as part of

5 "The Harry Potter stories are the most popular books in the Guantanamo Bay detention centre's library, the Pentagon has revealed. J. K. Rowling's tales of the teenage wizard were the most requested by terror suspects held at the high-security camp from among 3,500 titles available. . ." (*The Sunday Tasmanian*, 2006).

life, but also, I believe, it gave her great pleasure to feel that she did not need to suffer in order to have a baby, did not need to steal her father away from her mother or do away with her mother or allow herself to be invaded or penetrated in order to procure the prize. Although this girl had actually been adopted, adoption as a fantasy functioned to relax some of the pressures of psychological development with which she struggled. Indeed the symbol of adoption serves this function in the more oedipal meanings of Freud's family romance.

Freud's "adoption experience"

While Freud's (1909) treatise on the family romance is somewhat schematic, other writings reflect more clearly a preoccupation with the idea of two mothers. His letters to Fliess (Masson, 1985) and certain entries in "The Interpretation of Dreams" (1900) reveal that he himself had an "adoption experience" that was quite powerful and involved a great deal of trauma for him. As a small child Freud was placed in the care of a nanny who, after some time, was suddenly fired, arrested, and apparently sent to jail on charges that she had stolen from the family. This sudden disappearance probably was felt to replicate the sudden disappearance of the baby brother. Though Freud's theory and psychoanalytic investigations are primarily located within the oedipal era, much of what he discovered in his self-analysis was preoedipal (Blum, 1977), and much of the material from that era, as represented in his letters to Fliess and elsewhere, concern the conflicts and traumata of having lost two mothers, the biological mother and then the nanny (Schur, 1972). But the loss and adoption experiences were in fact not two but multiple. There was the loss of the mother's exclusive care with the birth of the baby brother, the probable further loss of the mother's attention with the death and mourning of the infant Julius, and the loss of the presence of the baby itself. Then there was the loss of the mother's actual care with the advent of the nanny and the sudden eternal disappearance of the nanny. Beyond this there was, no doubt, a pervasive decrease in attunement between Freud and his mother due to the time spent away from

100 each other and the losses they sustained, each in a distinct and separate way (Hardin & Hardin, 2000).[6]

Freud's interest in the theme of two mothers and his identification with the adoption experience is evident in his writings on Moses, Leonardo da Vinci and, of course, Oedipus—all great men with two or more mothers. While Freud's discovery of the Oedipus complex formed one of several bases for his theoretical and clinical work, the contributions of preoedipal life to pathology and character has been taken up almost as a corrective by most psychoanalytic schools deriving from Freud's work. In addition to Klein's paranoid schizoid position and Winnicott's good-enough mother, we have Balint's basic fault, Bion's containing object, Kohut's mirror transference, and Spotnitz's narcissistic transference and narcissistic defense. These theorists, and many others, have attempted to bring into greater focus the early dyadic period. Although Freud (1905) believed that the psychoanalytic armamentarium was not sufficient to the task of working with the psychoses, I think we are justified in also considering that Freud was resistant to approaching the preoedipal era for less objective reasons. Freud's resistances can be briefly pointed to in his professed lack of understanding of the "oceanic feeling" (1930); his peculiar emphasis on the child's need for the father, with a seeming blind spot regarding the importance of the mother as expressed, for example, in his paper on Leonardo Da Vinci (1910); or in his statement in "The Interpretation of Dreams" that the father is the only authority for the child "except in so far as the 'matriarchy' calls for a qualification of this assertion" (1900, fn. 1, p. 217). Yet, as stated above, Freud's earliest reconstructions in his self-analysis are from the preoedipal era and his adoption experience with the nanny, the subsequent loss of the nanny, and the re-adoption by Amalia, his biological mother.

In reading "Moses and Monotheism" one is struck by Freud's (1939) effort to understand the history of Judaism as linked to the history of not one Moses, but two distinct and separate founders with quite different personalities, each one offering a

---

6 The extraordinary love of Freud's mother for her golden boy from which Freud (1930) may have extrapolated his idea that the only human relationship without ambivalence is that of a mother for her son may be considered a reaction formation, particularly when one reads of Amalia's difficult and self-absorbed personality and of Freud's quite cool and even somatizing responses to her (Margolis, 1996; Jones, 1972; Schur, 1972).

different religion. Freud is describing a split in his people and a split in the parental figure—the father of the Jews. Whether or not such hypotheses have a bearing on the facts, it seems relevant to my own thoughts that Freud, at the end of his life, would be compelled to write of what could be understood as an object/self representation—a division in himself into two distinct and separate people reflecting the two mother imagoes from which his personality was born.[7]

The family romance is the mind's brilliant and complex solution to the dilemma of the long and protracted dependency of childhood. For even as it opens up a pathway for the possibility of development—the sexual desire for one parent and the conflictual casting aside of the other, which is the beginning of the journey to an appropriate object choice—it is clear that oedipal strivings also serve regressive needs. For in choosing one parent and doing away with the other, we are in fact restoring the magical dyadic system. In this context I think we can understand Oedipus's blinding of himself not only as symbolic of castration, but also as a turning away from the unwavering gaze into the mother's eyes, which is replicated in the gaze between lovers. When the lover is in *actuality* the parent, society exacts its price for breaking the brotherly bond, which, as Freud (1913) postulates in "Totem and Taboo," is the beginning of society.[8] The price is meted out according to the crime of regression; Oedipus may not return to the primitive omnipotence procured by seeing the mother's face.

In psychoanalytic terms we might say that Oedipus remains in the world of action; he has actualized his incestuous drives and now, by blinding himself, enacts in reality what was only metaphorically so—his inability to see himself or the world clearly. The separation from the early mother has cost Oedipus his

---

7 It may not be irrelevant to Freud's choice of topic that he himself was exposed to two "religious founders." His family and mother of course were Jewish, but the nanny was Catholic. Extremely religious, she included Freud in her devotional activities. As Freud's mother related to Freud, "She was always taking you to church. When you came home you used to preach, and tell us all about how God conducted His affairs" (Freud, 1954 qtd. in H. T. Hardin, 1987, p. 639).

8 Freud (1939) considers, in "Totem and Taboo," that taking the father's women is a breach of contract with the group, a contract signed in guilt for the brothers' murder of the father. This agreement between the guilty brothers is the beginning of a cooperative society.

real birthright, that is, the magical omnipotence conferred by a merged and secure state within the sphere of the mother's enlivening self.

The Greeks transformed Egypt's masculine sphinx into a feminine one. As such she is a magnificent symbol of a devouring female bent on destruction of those who seek to individuate. She is said to guard the city, ready to devour those who would rule without legitimacy (Ahl, 2008). I am suggesting that some of the force of the Oedipus story comes from the symbolic representation of the mother's murderous impulses and the child's self-attack as presented in Spotnitz's (Spotnitz & Meadow, 1995) theory of the narcissistic defense, whereby the frustrated child protects the mother image by attacking himself. In the first visitation of the Sphinx, Oedipus prevails and regains his lost omnipotence although it is split off from a process of reality testing and integration (Kohut, 1968) leaving him vulnerable to the lure of unconscious, delusional action. In other words, without an integrated omnipotence or grandiosity, Oedipus cannot reach an oedipal level that would allow him to "see" the other, i.e., the world and his place in it. Although the Sphinx has destroyed herself she returns, like the return of the repressed, in the form of a symptom, for the plague's attack on the city/body is surely a sign of her presence. Oedipus's undoing is his self-attack, which he unconsciously engineers by his decree of what will befall Laius's killer and then by his self-blinding and self-imposed exile. Starting as a displaced child he is driven blindly to enact a repetition of displacement that severs him from society and leaves him no place on this earth.

If we take Sophocles' *Oedipus* at face value, we cannot fail to see that surrounding the incest and murder is a story of fate, of hubris (grandiosity), of the highs and lows meted out by the world's love or hate of us. While the incest drama reflects our universal dilemma, the idea of the repetition compulsion and what Freud referred to as "fate neurosis" is perhaps a more inclusive theme.[9] Within that theme is the story not only of incest, but also of adoption and its oedipal and preoedipal symbolic meanings. By his

9 Freud (1920) actually used the term "fate compulsion" when referring to the affliction of those who "are pursued by a malignant fate or possessed by some daemonic power" (p. 20), but the idea was taken up by Deutsch (1930) and others as "fate neurosis."

choice of a hero dominated by a dual heritage, Freud did not entirely leave aside his own and our dichotomous adoption experience of early merger and separation culminating in a universal fantasy of two mothers and the fateful enactments to which the lack of an early, hallucinated omnipotence may give rise.

references Ahl, F. (2008), *Two Faces of Oedipus: Sophocles' Oedipus Tyrannus and Seneca's Oedipus.* Ithaca, NY: Cornell University Press.

Bion, W. R. (1962), *Learning from Experience.* London: Tavistock.

Bloch, D. (1974), Fantasy and the fear of infanticide. *The Psychoanalytic Review*, 61:5–31.

Blum, H. P. (1977), The prototype of preoedipal reconstruction. *Journal of the American Psychoanalytic Association,* 25:757–785.

Brinich, P. M. (1995), Psychoanalytic perspectives on adoption and ambivalence. *Psychoanalytic Psychology*, 12:181–199.

Deutsch, H. (1930), Hysterical fate neurosis. *Neuroses and Character Types.* New York: International Universities Press.

Dorpat, T. (1968), Regulatory mechanisms of the perceptual apparatus on involuntary physiological actions. *Journal of the American Psychoanalytic Association,* 16:319–334.

Freud, A. (1949), On certain difficulties in the preadolescent's relation to his parents. *Indications for Child Analysis and Other Papers.* Vol. 4 of *The Writings of Anna Freud.* New York: International Universities Press, 1968.

Freud, S. (1900), The interpretation of dreams. *Standard Edition.* London: Hogarth Press, 4 & 5.

Freud, S. (1905), On psychotherapy. *Standard Edition.* London: Hogarth Press, 7:255–268.

Freud, S. (1907), Delusions and dreams in Jensen's *Gradiva. Standard Edition.* London: Hogarth Press, 9:1–96.

Freud, S. (1909), Family romances. *Standard Edition.* London: Hogarth Press, 9:235–242.

Freud, S. (1910), Leonardo da Vinci and a memory of his childhood. *Standard Edition.* London: Hogarth Press, 11:57–138.

Freud, S. (1913), Totem and taboo. *Standard Edition.* London: Hogarth Press, 13:1–161.

Freud, S. (1920), Beyond the pleasure principle. *Standard Edition.* London: Hogarth Press, 18:3–64.

Freud, S. (1930), Civilization and its discontents. *Standard Edition.* London: Hogarth Press, 21:59–145.

Freud, S. (1939), Moses and monotheism: three essays. *Standard Edition.* London: Hogarth Press, 23:1–137.

Freud, S. (1954), *The Origins of Psychoanalysis. Letters to Wilhelm Fliess. Drafts and Notes: 1887–1902.* New York: Basic Books.

Green, A. (2001), The dead mother. *Life Narcissism, Death Narcissism.* Andrew Weller, trans. & ed. London: Free Association Books.

Hardin, H. T. (1987), On the vicissitudes of Freud's early mothering—I: early environment and loss. *Psychoanalytic Quarterly,* 56:628–644.

Hardin, H. T. & D. H. Hardin (2000), On the vicissitudes of early primary surrogate mothering II: loss of the surrogate mother and arrest of mourning. *Journal of the American Psychoanalytic Association,* 48:1229–1258.

Horner, T. M. & E. B. Rosenberg (1991), The family romance. *Psychoanalytic Psychology,* 8:131–148.

Jones, E. (1957), *The Last Phase 1919–1939.* Vol. III of *Sigmund Freud: Life And Work.* London: The Hogarth Press.

Jones, E. (1972), *The Young Freud 1856–1900.* Vol. I of *Sigmund Freud Life And Work.* London: The Hogarth Press.

Klein, M. (1946), Notes on some schizoid mechanisms. *International Journal of Psychoanalysis,* 27:99–110.

Kohut, H. (1968), The psychoanalytic treatment of narcissistic personality disorders—outline of a systematic approach. *Psychoanalytic Study of the Child,* 23:86–113.

Liedloff, J. (1986), *The Continuum Concept: In Search of Happiness Lost.* New York: Da Capo Press.

Mahler, M. S., F. Pine, & A. Bergman (1975), *The Psychological Birth of the Human Infant: Symbiosis and Individuation.* New York: Basic Books.

Margolis, D. (1996), *Freud and His Mother: Preoedipal Aspects of Freud's Personality.* Northvale, NJ: Jason Aronson.

Masson, J. M., trans. & ed. (1985), *The Complete Letters of Sigmund Freud to Wilhelm Fliess,* 1887–1904. Cambridge: Harvard University Press.

Perruchot, H. (1958), *Cezanne*. Cleveland: World Publishing Company.

Rewald, J. (1968), *Paul Cezanne: A Biography*. New York: Schocken Books.

Schur, M. (1972), *Freud: Living and Dying*. New York: International Universities Press, Inc.

Spitz, R. (1983), The primal cavity: a contribution to the genesis of perception and its role for psychoanalytic theory. *Dialogues from Infancy: Selected Papers*. New York: International Universities Press, Inc.

Spotnitz, H. & P. W. Meadow (1976), *Treatment of the Narcissistic Neuroses*. Rev. ed. Northvale, NJ: Jason Aronson, Inc.

The Sunday Tasmanian (2006), Harry's a hit at Guantanamo. September 17. http://www.news.com.au/story/0,23599,204254801-3762,00.html

Winnicott, D. W. (1945), Primitive emotional development. *International Journal of Psychoanalysis,* 26:137–143.

Winnicott, D. W. (1953), Transitional objects and transitional phenomena: a study of the first not-me possession. *International Journal of Psychoanalysis*, 34:89–97.

55 Bethune St.
New York, NY 10014
josiop@earthlink.net

Consciousness and interpretation in modern psychoanalysis

June Bernstein

This paper discusses how some of the reflective techniques of modern analysis and the tendency to avoid anything ego-oriented may keep analysts and patients locked into the status quo phase of analysis. The fear of losing the patient may motivate some therapists to be so careful that patients are not helped to recognize and move beyond their repetitions. In order to reach the stages of progressive communication and cooperation, patients must be given the chance to know themselves through ego-syntonic explanations and to consciously decide to work with the analyst.

Freud (1923) revised the topographical model of the mind when he realized that, due to its defenses, a good part of the executive apparatus (the ego) was unconscious and therefore behaved like the id. "Where id was ego should be" became the aim of psychoanalysis. When we ask people to say whatever comes to mind, we have an aim—and that aim is to make what is unconscious (or at least pre-conscious) conscious by verbalizing it. Like Freud, we believe that making something conscious deprives it of its power to motivate behavior and gives more control. Freud relied on interpretations addressed to the patient's conscious ego, as do most schools of thought at present no matter what their theoretical orientation. The practice that most noticeably separates modern analysis from other psychoanalytic schools is the use of interventions that depart from the rational, the use of what we call "emotional communications."

However, in our dedication to emotional communication and to such modern analytic interventions as joining, mirroring, following the contact, and asking object-oriented questions, we may be overlooking some of the advantages of interpretation as well as other more traditional and widely used appeals to the rational ego. Emotional communications are far more powerful than explanations, but they can represent a real threat to some egos. A patient who joined a group became extremely agitated by the emotional communications that were made there. Although many people are energized by emotional arousal, this person couldn't handle it. She became seriously overstimulated, was convinced the group and the group analyst were dangerous to her, and took a vacation from the group. She was both extremely fragile and highly intelligent. She could make use of explanations that addressed her rational mind and didn't stir up an overwhelming amount of feeling. Freud (1915) says that most defenses are instituted against feelings: "To suppress the development of affect is the true aim of repression . . ." (p. 178). We tread on dangerous ground when we arouse emotions that the person is trying to defend against.

conscious resistance

Sometimes the patient's conscious mind may be the source of resistance. That is one of the reasons why it is important to ask someone, whose problem may seem obvious, whether he wants to change anything. Surprisingly often the person hesitates and reveals he is not interested in any change in himself. The aim seems to be to change the environment.

One patient was discontented with the lack of respect and prestige he had at work and in his dealings with women. However, he considered the demands of work and of women to be based on values that were shallow and contemptible. He did not consciously want to change anything about himself; he wanted the world to improve its values.

People may have many conscious resistances to being successful; they may dislike "successful types." They don't want to be pushy, aggressive, competitive, and striving. They do not want to conform; they want to remain absent-minded, late, rude, or oppositional—to continue as they are but not be penalized for it. They may see themselves as lovable eccentrics, proud of their individuality and of the sensitivity that results in their making trouble for themselves.

Our first job with so-called character disorders may be to arouse the conscious ego's willingness to relinquish some problem behavior that is undermining the person's ability to thrive and enjoy life. Patients who wish to get more love, have to be willing to be more lovable.

conscious effort

Often patients say they want to feel better. Spotnitz was known to suggest that they consciously change their behavior to resemble that of people who actually do feel good, and that the feelings may follow. Meadow was famous for insisting that depressed people try to look cheerful. She'd say "Smile!" when she saw one of her depressed protégées looking glum.

Spotnitz once told a training group that people who were always depressed might benefit from taking an antidepressant in order to experience what it was like not to be depressed. When they got accustomed to it, their resistance to giving up the drug could be resolved.

strengthening the ego

What are we trying to accomplish when we provide an environment in which the patient's ego is insulated, or "held," when we concern ourselves with joining the ego so that its defenses will be preserved, when we ask questions that are "object-oriented" so that the patient's ego will not be threatened, or when we foster a narcissistic transference so the patient won't have to deal with an alien presence? We are shielding the ego like a delicate plant in the interest of strengthening it so that it will not give up when it is stimulated, opposed, narcissistically wounded, or otherwise stressed. The end product is always meant to be a stronger ego, one that can maintain itself in the teeth of "the slings and arrows of outrageous fortune."

Spotnitz (1988) sometimes described the job of analysis as the strengthening of an ego. His monograph on "Treatment of a

Pre-schizophrenic Adolescent" was subtitled "Case Presentation on the Reconstruction of a Psychotic Ego."

the ego and aggression

Freud (1920) noted that the ego controls the approaches to motility. He also noted that the individual survives the death instinct by directing it outward, a feat that is accomplished through the use of the musculature. In fact, he believed that any action that uses the musculature has the aggression of the projected death instinct as a source of its energy. According to Freud (1940),

> So long as the instinct operates internally as a death instinct, it remains silent; it only comes to our notice when it is diverted outward as an instinct of destruction. It seems to be essential for the preservation of the individual that this diversion should occur: the muscular apparatus serves this purpose. (p. 150)

Since many of our patients founder when faced with their own or another's aggression, they restrict their movements, both in thought and deed. Many analysts try to circumvent the existence of innate aggression by offering other solutions for its genesis or by declaring that aggression is not really aggressive (Sternbach, 1975). Unfortunately, Freud (1940b) makes very clear what he means by aggression, and he does not mean a neutral energy that may be applied to constructive or destructive goals. He means something destructive that, with luck, may be fused with something constructive so that the result is an amalgam of good and evil. He says, "Modifications in the proportions of the fusion between the instincts have the most tangible results. A surplus of sexual aggressiveness will turn a lover into a sex-murderer, while a sharp diminution in the aggressive factor will make him a bashful lover" (p. 149).

One of the outcomes of strengthening the ego is better control of aggression and less need for radical and debilitating defenses against it. This applies to the person doing treatment as well as the one receiving it.

strengthening the ego of the analyst

Some students of modern analysis are so afraid of making the patient angry that they are unable to explore what is going on in the treatment. They fear any investigation would be perceived by the patient as an attack. Some cannot even mention that the patient owes them money unless the patient raises the issue first.

A student who was made uncomfortable by a patient's detailed description of his anal sexual behavior hesitated to follow the suggestion that she ask why he was telling her about it in every session. After all, patients are supposed to "say everything." However, analysts are supposed to analyze everything. After the treatment-destructive stage and the status quo resistance, modern analysts presumably work on the resistance to progress. One resistance on the part of the analyst is the fear of asking ego-oriented questions or of offering interpretations. Analysts may know what they are feeling but are afraid to say anything that might be construed as an attack. This often leads to a status quo stalemate.

unconscious or unspoken?

The way to make the unconscious conscious, according to Freud (1923), is to make it preconscious (p. 20). In the preconscious state something may be known but not spoken. Frequently patients and students hold back on thoughts and opinions of which they are perfectly aware. Although unconscious motives also exist, to get at them the analyst has to work first on getting the patient to tell what he knows.

With preoedipal patients, material is often unspoken rather than unconscious. Freud believed that repression was the defense employed against sexual and aggressive wishes belonging to the Oedipus complex. We may therefore assume that it is not the primary defense used by preoedipal patients dealing with other conflicts. In some cases, material is being withheld in order to protect the object.

When Meadow (1987) assured a doctoral candidate who was unable to write her thesis that she was not up to doctoral standards, the patient directed her rage at the analyst giving Meadow all the negative impressions she'd ever had of her. In this case, and in others like it, the angry thoughts about the analyst are not unconscious but unspoken. Meadow's was a double-barreled emotional communication since it precluded the unconscious satisfaction the patient was getting in defeating the analyst (after Meadow's intervention, if the patient failed in writing her dissertation, the analyst would be proved right instead of defeated) as well as getting her to voice her unexpressed rage.

formulating an interpretation

Getting the patient to verbalize the unspoken preconscious tells us a lot, but not as much as we learn from the patient's repetitive feeling states. For patients to be willing to consider their repetitive feeling states as self-perpetuating and to work on the reasons motivating them to repeat, we have to formulate an understanding (an interpretation) of what is going on.

A patient who had a life history of being unappreciated was very frustrated and frequently full of bottled-up anger. Recently she arrived for a session full of grievances against me. She claimed that I undermined her confidence, would disapprove of a project she wanted to undertake, and was so impatient when hearing about her frustrations at work that she couldn't even tell me about them anymore. All of this would seem to suggest that she needed to discharge her hate so as not to turn it against herself. However, since I had known her for a very long time, I recognized that something else was also going on. The session before this one had been unusually productive, and she had left feeling elated. It occurred to me that she was having some anxiety about relinquishing her usual feeling state of frustration. I knew, because she had talked about it before, that feeling elated frightened her. It seemed more productive to talk about why she needed to restore her usual negative feeling-state than to ask object-oriented questions about why I would frustrate her. My formulation of what was going on raised considerable resistance. She came late to the next two sessions to punish me and to prove that my intervention was harmful. Patients fight hard to retain the status quo. In this case I had to refuse the invitation to engage in a negative interaction because her resistance was to having positive feelings. She was unaware of her need to perpetuate a certain kind of feeling state, and it required conscious effort on her part to give up an action and engage in analyzing it. Eventually the analyst has to use the patient's contacts and repetitions to develop an impression of their meaning and to formulate an interpretation.

ego-syntonic interpretations

Interpretation has a bad name among modern analysts because it is considered an attack on the ego. However, not all interpretations are destructive or unpleasant. Often the analyst provides an ego-syntonic explanation amounting to an interpretation. In such cases patients may feel listened to and understood.

One patient used his time with me to express dissatisfaction with one or another aspect of his life. He considered me a failure because I had not helped him to feel better. I pointed out that he wasn't allowing himself to feel good. He was attacking himself by attacking the circumstances and people in his life. I recalled that he once told me that his misery as a child had frustrated his parents and had made them feel like failures. He was repeating his past in a way that continued to deprive him of joy. He needed to permit himself to feel more pleasure in his life.

This interpretation focused on how he was harming himself and not on the subterranean pleasure he was possibly getting in frustrating me. It is sometimes more useful to interpret what the patient is accomplishing with himself rather than how he is affecting the transference object. Previous explorations of what he was doing to me had led to the admission that he got pleasure in making people feel uncomfortable. His wish to frustrate others and make them feel like failures was conscious. What he was unaware of was how mean he was to himself.

The interpretation that focuses on what the patient is doing to himself rather than to the object is true to the modern psychoanalytic understanding of the pre-object phase of development when self and object are merged. The patient's only real object is himself; the other is only an aspect of the self. He treats others the way he treats himself. We have a choice of going with an interpretation of what he is doing to himself or focusing on what he is doing to the object. In modern analysis we tend to focus on the object, an approach that can be very helpful to schizophrenic patients who ignore the object and bottle up aggression. However, ultimately, the narcissistic patient is more interested in himself than he is in others.

Explanations that appeal to the rational ego can be considered object-oriented interventions—the object to which the explanation is addressed is the patient's ego. Interpretations are often formulated in universal terms, like the Oedipus complex, fear of separation, or universally existing sexual and aggressive wishes, rather than belonging to the patient alone. (The Jungian archetypes may arouse little anxiety because they are part of a universal "collective unconscious" so the patient is not personally responsible.) Such interpretations arouse less tension than emotional communications addressed specifically to the patient's dynamics.

confrontation, clarification, interpretation, and working through

It is not possible to offer an explanation of any sort when the patient is in a state of resistance. At those times the analyst has to stick to exploration, mirroring, joining, and emotional communications. However, since patients are not always in a state of resistance, sometimes it is right to tell them things. It helps if we know what to tell them, which is the art of interpretation.

There is usually no big mystery about the repetition, which the patient will continue to demonstrate in the transference and in his life until the analyst becomes aware of it. At first, all the analyst has to do is remark on it. This is what Greenson (1967) calls "confrontation" although it does not have to be very confrontational. It can convey an awareness, acceptable to the ego, of how the patient repeats certain behaviors that are not in his own interest and thereby defeats himself or makes his life less enjoyable. The clarification step then comes from what the patient has to say about it—the history of the behavior, its rewards, the memories attached to it, and fears of relinquishing it. The analyst knows enough about the patient and about the unconscious at this point to be able to contribute further acceptable understanding of the purpose of the repetition (the interpretation).

The "working through" consists of dealing with, and further elaborating, the meaning of the repetition, whenever it recurs in the transference or in the patient's report of his life.

managing countertransference feelings

Our countertransference may provoke us to behave toward the patient as people do in his outside life. However, we do not want to replicate the way in which he usually interacts with others. While it is important to know what feelings the patient is creating in us, it is equally important not to use them hastily to discharge our own tensions. Spotnitz (1969) describes how in order to create an ego the afferent impulses have to be held within the psyche and not immediately discharged by the efferent neurons (p. 64). To create our analytic egos, we have to learn how to hold the tension of the countertransference within our psyches. We have to master our own anxiety and refrain from talking unless we have some therapeutic motive in mind.

resistance to progress and to cooperation

In the relationship-destructive and status quo phases of the analysis, we rely primarily on reflective techniques like joining and mirroring (Spotnitz, 1969). As we start to work on the resistance to progress (the state at which most of our single-case studies begin), we try to figure out what is motivating the patient to maintain his repetition and what might move him in the direction of making progress and engaging with the analyst in the cooperative venture of analyzing as opposed to merely enacting, repeating, or feeling comfortable and understood.

It is only when the resistances to progress and cooperation have been at least partially resolved that anything like a therapeutic or working alliance can be expected. It is at this point that we can begin to work with the person's available ego and with interpretations. It may be bumpy at first. When we bring a repetitive pattern to their attention, patients (especially if they are students of modern psychoanalysis) may demand to know how being aware of their repetition is going to help them. Now that they know, what are they supposed to do about it? Freud (1919) discussed whether, when an analyst has analyzed something, it is his duty to synthesize it. According to Freud, it is not necessary because the mind itself automatically performs this function. He says of the torn mind: "As we analyse it and remove the resistances, it grows together; the great unity which we call his ego fits into itself all the instinctual impulses which before had been split off and held apart from it" (p. 161). Patients don't have to worry about what to do with the knowledge they get in analysis, providing they really "get" it, it will become part of the coherent ego that has been compromised by defenses against knowing.

Because nobody ever gives up a resistance entirely, the old resistances tend to recur whenever a new phase begins. Both analyst and patient are drawn to revive old interactions, partly because they are comfortable. One of my patients who is working on being a *mensch* still falls into the routine of being a baby, and I fall into the role of being the grownup. We are both forgetting our new aim, that she be an adult. Resistances interfere with our being two adults working cooperatively together.

termination

For Spotnitz (1969), resistance to cooperation and to termination are the last two phases of treatment. Modern analysts take their time about terminating. They tend to believe that as long as the patient is still getting something from it, there is no need to end the analysis. They are so aware of the tendency to end relationships prematurely that they don't waste much time worrying about their going on too long. There is a "'Til death do us part" aspect to many modern analyses.

However, since the deaths of Meadow and Spotnitz, there has been a certain amount of talk about the gains of being on one's own. Colleagues sometimes say they notice a greater freedom to be themselves professionally, to adopt new points of view, and to be the grownups taking responsibility for themselves and for the next generation.

Perhaps the next generation will come to grips with the question of the termination.

references   Freud, S. (1915), The unconscious. *Standard Edition.* London: Hogarth Press, 14:168–204.

Freud, S. (1919), Lines of advance in psycho-analytic psychotherapy. *Standard Edition*. London: Hogarth Press, 17:157–168.

Freud, S. (1920), Beyond the pleasure principle. *Standard Edition*. London: Hogarth Press, 18:3-64.

Freud, S. (1923), The ego and the id. *Standard Edition*. London: Hogarth Press, 19:3–66.

Freud, S. (1940a), Splitting of the ego in the process of defence. *Standard Edition*. London: Hogarth Press, 23:271–278.

Freud, S. (1940b), An outline of psycho-analysis. *Standard Edition*. London: Hogarth Press, 23:141–207.

Greenson, R. (1967), *The Technique and Practice of Psychoanalysis*. New York: International Universities Press.

McKay, N. (1989), *Motivation and Explanation: An Essay on Freud's Philosophy of Science*. Madison, CT: International Universities Press.

Meadow, P. (1987), The myth of the impersonal analyst. *Modern Psychoanalysis,* 12:131–150.

Spotnitz, H. (1969), *Modern Psychoanalysis of the Schizophrenic Patient: Theory of the Technique*. New York: Grune & Stratton.

Spotnitz, H. (1988), Treatment of a pre-schizophrenic adolescent. *Modern Psychoanalysis,* 13:5–208.

Sternbach, O. (1975), Aggression, the death drive and the problem of sadomasochism: a reinterpretation of Freud's second drive theory. *International Journal of Psychoanalysis,* 56:321–333.

16 Gerlach Place
Larchmont, NY 10538
junstein@verizon.net

Mary Shelley's *Frankenstein:* an orphaned author's dream and journey toward integration

Barbara D'Amato

The author examines unconscious links between Mary Shelley's internal conflicts and life experiences and what may have been their manifestations in the fictionalized characters she created in *Frankenstein*. The dream that inspired Shelley's *Frankenstein* is also analyzed as an account of her repetitive psychic struggles and a rich source of imagery driving the development of her novel. The author proposes that both dream and novel may have functioned to provide Shelley with a source of discharge, solace, and eventual acceptance of her losses.

> In narcissism, the search for union with another person can be seen as a longing for reconnection with a missing part of the self.
>
> Phyllis Meadow (2000)

Orphans are children who have lost one or both parents to death. Even if surrogate parents, such as stepparents, familial, or adoptive parents, emerge, such individuals are considered orphans throughout their lives. There has been little research into the emotional conflicts and psychic experiences of orphans. Since 2000, however, research on adoptees—children relinquished by a biological mother and subsequently placed in the care of another parent or set of parents—has begun to proliferate (Brodzinsky, 1990, p. 12). This research has focused on investigating conflicts that deal with a capacity for emotional connection and includes numerous studies of maternal representations and attachment (Priel, Kantor, & Besser, 2000; Steele et al., 2003; Verrier, 2003; Powell & Afifi, 2005; Warshaw, 2006).

The literature on orphans and adoptees consistently finds that young children who have been separated from their biological parents live with a sense of loss and are often developmentally at risk (Bowlby, 1940; A. Freud & Burlingham, 1944; Kirk, 1964; Ainsworth, 1967; Brodzinsky et al., 1984; Robertson & Robertson, 1989; Brodzinsky, 1990). Both adoption researchers working empirically and clinicians working with the unconscious communications of adopted patients in the treatment room would agree that the experience of relinquishment at a very early age has psychic consequences (Wieder, 1977; Brinich,1990; Partridge,1991; Verrier,1993; Charon,1994; Lifton,1994; Hertz,1996; Quinodoz,1996; Silverstein & Kaplan,1982; Hafetz, 2005). The conflict around connection is often at the core of the orphan's psychic experience. The unconscious conflicts and psychic experiences of loss and of longing for connection are captured and revealed in the orphaned character of Mary Shelley's fictional story *Frankenstein*. The bond between the story's characters and the author who created them and the author's dream are explored in this paper.

writers' dreams

Timeless novels like *Jane Eyre, Wuthering Heights,* and *Oliver Twist* depict tales of impoverished orphans who, through various events, transcend their unfortunate predicaments and meet with good fortune. These transformations often involve a dream or a series of dreams (Thomas, 1990). Authors' dreams frequently inspire their creative stories, unconsciously imposing the author's personal conflicts upon the characters. Gothic writers in particular, according to Thomas, "attributed their [stories'] origins to dreams, often to emphasize a failure on the part of even the writers to understand and control the forces that drove their narratives" (p. 72). Mary Shelley (1996) is one such author, having created the classic story *Frankenstein*—and perhaps literature's most infamous orphan—after an inspirational dream about a terrifying fiend. Thomas says, "her dream text may be seen as expressing a desire for a scientific language to identify and explain human psychology" (p. 96).

Freud (1900), a gifted writer, revealed himself and his early conflicts in "The Interpretation of Dreams" as he analyzed his own dream material. Well aware that dreams disclose the dreamer, Freud took heed not to expose himself completely when he used his personal conflicts to demonstrate his theory. In a reference to his interpretation of "The Botanical Monograph" (p. 169) he states: "I shall not pursue the interpretation of this dream any further, but will merely indicate the direction in which it lay" (p. 173). Freud clearly avoided a complete interpretation, which may have led him to uncover many of his own early conflicts (Lacan, 1954-55; Blum, 1979; Meadow, 1984; Margolis, 1996; van den Berg, 1997). However, his proviso underscores Freud's (1900, 1907) belief that writers betray who they are, their core conflicts and well-guarded secrets revealed as they emerge in dreams and literary works.

Thomas (1990) in *Dreams of Authority*—his investigative study of the links between nineteenth-century English gothic novels, psychoanalytic theory, and dream interpretation—comments on the juxtaposition of Mary Shelley's intuitive understanding of her own dream and her character Frankenstein's blatant and fatal lack of understanding:

> Frankenstein fails to realize what Mary realizes in her introduction [to the novel]: in the modern world, human beings are not spoken to in dreams; they are speaking to themselves. The dream does not invade the dreamer; it is invented by the dreamer. (p. 90)

As they worked through their own unconscious conflicts, some authors produced classic works that reflected an anticipation of Freudian theory. Mary Shelley's creative writing demonstrates such an attempt, and is one author's desire to understand herself through unconscious dream material and fictional/autobiographical orphaned characters.

Mary Shelley, author, dreamer, orphan: a process of working through

The nineteenth-century writer Mary Shelley was the daughter of two famous, radical authors, the philosopher William Godwin and renowned feminist Mary Wollstonecraft. Shelley knew and admired her parents' writings and spent time studying the works of both as she created *Frankenstein* (1996), or *The Modern Prometheus* as it was originally titled. Initially his mistress, Mary eventually married the already accomplished Percy Shelley. Surrounded by successful writers, she believed herself an imitator rather than an original writer (Thomas, 1990). Although she was a highly educated woman, an ardent reader of the classics, and proficient in five languages, she doubted her abilities as a writer. Describing herself as a copious dreamer, Mary questioned her skill as a writer claiming "my dreams were at once more fantastic and agreeable than my writings" (p. 169). In a preface to *Frankenstein* (added to the story in 1831, 13 years after the original publication), Shelley briefly describes the dream (or daydream) that motivated her fantastic story:

> When I placed my head upon my pillow, I did not sleep, nor could I be said to think. My imagination, unbidden, possessed and guided me, gifting the successive images that arose in my mind with a vividness far beyond the usual bounds of reverie. I saw—with eyes shut but acute mental vision—I saw the pale student of unhallowed arts kneeling beside the thing he had just put together. I saw the hideous phantasm of a man stretched out, and then, on the working of some powerful engine, show signs of life, stir with an uneasy, half vital motion. . . . His success would terrify the artist; he would rush away from his odious handy-work, horror-stricken. He would hope that left to itself, the slight spark of life which he had communicated would fade . . . into dead matter; and he might sleep in the belief that the silence of the grave would quench for ever the transient existence of the hideous corpse which he had looked upon as the cradle of life. (p. 172)

This dream may have been Mary's solution to the problem of creating fiction that could compete with that of Percy Shelley and Lord Byron. The three had engaged in a ghost-story writing contest, while vacationing in Geneva. Mary struggled relentlessly "to think of a story" (1996, p. 171) that was worthy. She may also have struggled with a conflict about writing itself. Did she want to compete with her husband in the literary world of men? Or did she want to produce babies as a way to fulfill her creative energies? The dichotomy between producing children and/or producing fiction would remain an active struggle throughout Shelley's life (Smith, 2000). Both are means to achieve a common end—immortality.

Additionally, Mary may well have considered writing as a link to, and perpetuation of, a generation of writers. She may have imagined herself an heiress to that tradition. Both her parents lived unorthodox lives and were authors who chronicled radical points of view. They were each staunch opponents of the institution of marriage and only agreed to marry as a means to avoid Mary's bastardization. Wollstonecraft wrote on women's rights and the oppressed, while Godwin wrote several controversial books that attacked nineteenth-century aristocracy and supported social anarchy (Smith, 2000). Female writers were rare in the early 1800s, and Mary may have been ambivalent about taking on such a masculine endeavor as her mother before her had done. Yet she seemed to yearn for the gratification writing a book offered as well as the opportunity it would give her not only to equal both her parents, but also perhaps surpass them. Choosing just the right story was crucial in Mary's young mind. On an unconscious level writing her novel may have symbolized more than a writing contest with her husband. The fantasy of writing a successful story may have contained aggressive aspects of both oedipal strivings to outshine and replace her mother, and preoedipal desires to become her mother, whom she had tragically lost just days after her birth. This resonates with Almond's (1998) ideas that link Mary's absent mother with her own feelings of murderousness and unlovability, "while rejection by her father left Mary with the notion that her unacceptable sexual, and . . . incestuous wishes were 'monstrous' to her" (p. 177).

When she finally selected the concept for her chronicle *Frankenstein,* Shelley made more than a conscious decision to write. She appears to have unconsciously revealed some of her deepest feelings about life, death, and connection through her characters.

writing or mothering: two acts of procreation

As Mary's creative energy flowed into her writing of *Frankenstein,* Mary's body was enacting life and death, with several successive yet unsuccessful pregnancies and births (Moers, 1974). Miscarriages and neonatal mortalities can be viewed psychoanalytically as physical manifestations of Mary's conflict. Percy was still married to his first wife at the time of Mary's initial pregnancy wherein the baby lived only a few days. Over the course of the next several years, Mary would miscarry and lose three more children in early childhood. Mary was familiar with death. She was herself an orphan, her mother having died due to complications of childbirth when Mary was eleven days old (Shelley, 1996). Mary's half sister and Percy's first wife both committed suicide. Shelley, of course, knew nothing of Freud and psychoanalytic theory since she predates them both. Her internal conflicts surrounding motherhood and mothering were, however, being processed within this story on purely unconscious and perhaps somatic levels, beginning with her dream. Victor Frankenstein abandons his creation, making Victor a would-be-mother who relinquished his role. This thread in the story may suggest that writing is safer than actually giving birth. Yet bearing and losing children enacts Mary's repetition and appears to have been a necessity in her life. *Frankenstein* may have simply been Shelley's record of that life. Yet, *Frankenstein,* like all literary work, gave Shelley eternal life.

Miscarriage and infant death are solutions that may presumably rid a mother of an unwanted, or feared, fetus and child. Giving birth to a monster is an unconscious fear many pregnant women experience and is detailed in Almond's (1998) clinical paper on the subject. Her apt observations from pregnant women in treatment reveal the meaning of their unconscious fantasies about producing a monster. These fantasies are related to deeply buried worries about the incestuous meaning of babies and the aggressiveness of the mother-to-be. Aggression is projected onto the growing fetus and manifests itself as fear of a potential, in utero demon (p. 181). Almond further proposes that Mary may have believed any child she produced would inherit the repressed, hated, and destructive parts of herself. While being pregnant seemed to appeal to her, Mary seemed more uncertain about the nature of the progeny she would deliver (Shelley, 1996, p. 173). She had similar fears regarding her ability to write.

the story unfolds: merger, loss, and death

Frankenstein, Mary's "hideous progeny," begins with her preface (added in 1831), alluding to her inspirational dream. The rest of the story takes place on a ship that has become frozen among icebergs in unknown northern waters. The tale unfolds like Russian nesting dolls, each character's first-person narrative moving closer to the core of the author's psyche, revealing the speaker's deepest conflicts. First is a series of letters from a young explorer, Walton, to his beloved sister. Walton, on an ambitious expedition to the North Pole, yearns in vain to meet his true soulmate. He unexpectedly encounters Victor Frankenstein (who is roving the earth to escape the monster) in the icy arctic waters, where Walton's vessel has been trapped. Walton's grandiose desire to reach the North Pole, as well as an unbearable yearning to connect with another similar companion, have landed him and his crew in a perilous situation.

Again in a first-person narrative, Victor tells Walton his story, climaxing with the monster's creation. Victor's visions of grandeur, in which he hoped to make great contributions to his field of science and medicine, drove him to work relentlessly to discover the secret of creation. The fiend has been searching for Victor and has followed him to the trapped ship. When Victor finally reunites with the demon from whom he has fled, the nameless fiend recounts his story. It is a story of epic proportion, beginning with his abandonment and struggles to survive. By secretly observing a family, the fiend "learns" how to be human. But his heart-wrenching desire for acceptance and love is repeatedly denied due to his deformed, frightening appearance.

Mary Shelley, Walton, Victor Frankenstein, and his monster are all orphans, motherless creatures. Each of them is longing and searching for connection: the struggle against isolation is central to each repetitive story. As in a dream, all of the figures in *Frankenstein* appear to represent some psychical piece of Shelley. The story, continually told in the first person, keeps the reader always closely linked to the character. At times it is not clear exactly *who* is speaking, leaving the reader with a sense of uncertainty about the boundaries separating these characters from one another and from Shelley herself.

Shelley's conflict via literary criticism

Various literary critics describe *Frankenstein* as a story of procreation, one in which Victor Frankenstein usurps the creative, reproductive powers hitherto only experienced by women. Thomas (1990), for example, discusses "the horror of his [Frankenstein's] desire to create a man by himself—without a mother," (p. 89). Small (1973), however, refers to the story as a disguised biographical sketch of Mary's husband Percy. It is also considered a study of the parental responsibilities of a father to a son, the result of Oedipal relationships in the family, and a portrayal of the two sides of man—good and evil (Levine, 1973). Moers (1974) interprets it as a birth-myth, based on Mary's own experiences of motherhood, and a study of the "divided self." From a psychoanalytic perspective, Frankenstein and the monster can be viewed as two aspects of the same man. They both may be aspects of the author as well.

Gilbert and Gubar (1979), in *Madwoman in the Attic,* flirt with psychoanalytic theory in their suggestion that Mary's unconscious feelings for her mother may have influenced her writing of *Frankenstein.* They report that Mary frequented her mother's grave, where she studied and rendezvoused with Percy. Gilbert and Gubar also connect *Frankenstein* to Milton's *Paradise Lost,* a story with which Mary was infatuated. Mary's teenage pregnancy and subsequent marriage to Percy led her famous father to disown her. These two authors compare Mary to Eve. Eve was the inferior one, created, not in the "image and likeness of God," but from Adam's rib. Mary was renounced by her father, the second wife to her husband, the mother of three dead children, and considered herself a second-rate writer. Mary's young life was rich with failures and rejections.

Shelley's conflict from a psychoanalytic perspective

Numerous authors have analyzed the story of *Frankenstein* from the perspective of Mary Shelley's life. Mary's actual life occurrences have been linked to a diagnostic manual of explanations and inferences that suggest some of the psychic consequences of those experiences, which were artistically projected onto fictional characters, particularly Victor and his monster. Almond (1998) suggests that Mary's deepest conflicts surrounded her unconscious belief that she herself was Dr. Frankenstein's monster. Almond argues that Mary, rendered motherless by a physician who, just days after Mary's birth, was unable to save her mother, "Wreaks a painful revenge on doctors who bungle their work" (p. 776). *Frankenstein* is a story portraying a physician who systematically loses each and every person he has ever loved, making revenge a palpable theme.

Collings (2000) provides one of the richest psychoanalytic perspectives of this literary work as it pertains to the author and also presents a Lacanian interpretation of the universal conflict the monster embodies. All three—Shelley, Victor, and the creature—are indelibly merged and interchangeable throughout the tale, revealing various levels of disaster involved with bearing and losing a child and losing a mother, and also revealing the unconscious meaning of the heinous side of our own humanness reflected in Lacan's imaginary order.[1] The imaginary order contains a world of illusion and is essentially narcissistic and alienating. It contains the mirror image, the double, and a denial of separateness—all critical to Shelley's story.

As a child moves out of the imaginary, he approaches Lacan's symbolic order, which arises with language and contains a social order and kinship. At this stage the child begins to understand that he is separate from his mother. It is an experience of loss (Hurst, 1999; Collings, 2000). Victor tried to maintain the imaginary as he created the monster, his double and his early maternal object, *within* the social order of reality, or in denial of it. Psychically, he disavowed loss and separation from the early self-object with his attempt to recreate it through the monster.[2] Sadly, his endeavor was destined to fail.

Collings teases out the meaning of Victor's repulsion and fear of the creature as it enters his bedchamber upon becoming infused with life. He relates this scene to the Lacanian mirror stage in which the child sees itself for the first time in a mirror and erroneously believes he is a unified whole. At this stage a child has the first inklings that he is separate from the mother. When Victor views the monster, pieced together from fragments of dead corpses, standing before him in the illusion of a unified whole, it is more than his psyche can tolerate. Through his creation Victor has transcended the imaginary order and

1 I would like to thank Dr. William Hurst for his help in clarifying Lacan's imaginary and symbolic orders.

2 Lacanian theory posits that the imaginary and symbolic orders continuously overlap (Fink, 1997; Nobus, 2000), while Collings surmises that Victor could not *fully* exist in both registers simultaneously.

observes before him a unified whole that is really a *falsely* unified, disjointed perception. The creature represents that which Victor denies—his own fragmented, alienated, and monstrous self. The result is a universal and psychic perception of motherlessness and of being entirely alone.

Many authors have elaborated upon the theme of motherlessness and how it may have affected Mary's self-image and sexual identity. Godwin was distraught when Wollstonecraft died and could not adequately raise Mary alone (Smith, 2000). Yet he adored Mary and showered her with attention, while repeatedly reminding her of *his* loss. When Shelley was four years old, Godwin married Mary Jane Clairmont. The newlyweds quickly produced a son named William, Shelley's stepbrother, who features prominently in *Frankenstein,* and is the monster's first victim (more psychic revenge). Mary eventually went to live with relatives because Clairmont believed Mary and Godwin were too close (Smith, 2000). Mary surely felt betrayed and rejected by her father. At the time of Mary's elopement with Percy, Godwin disowned her. In later years they reconciled after she married Percy, but Godwin's harshness persisted. After Mary lost her first child, Godwin advised her to be stoic as she pleaded with him for comfort. Her ambivalence about writing and about producing children was an intricate conflict that can be examined on numerous psychic levels and was related to the meaning she placed on her own motherlessness.

Modern psychoanalysts (Spotnitz & Meadow, 1976; Spotnitz, 1981; Spotnitz, 1985) consider psychic conflict in terms of preoedipal disturbances, which arise at a time prior to language, essentially during the first two years of life. When conflicts occur in the very early life of an individual, there are inadequate pathways for tension reduction and discharge. An infant can experience narcissistic injuries based upon its perceptions of its environment/self and the tension states these perceptions arouse. At this stage of development the environment and the "other" are not experienced as separate objects, but as parts of the object field of the mind (Meadow, 1989, 2000). Both internal and external sensations and experiences are understood as parts of the self. When there is inadequate tension reduction, the developing infant can become overloaded with stimulation, both pleasurable and unpleasurable. These disturbances can be experienced somatically. They hold no roots in the language of the child or later adult, yet they will be re-experienced, psychically, again and again, unconsciously manifesting themselves.

Psychoanalytically, *Frankenstein* can be understood as Shelley's wish to re-create that part of her lost when her mother died, potentially an unconscious attempt to become more fully integrated. Meadow (2000) says that "in narcissism, the search for union with another person can be seen as a longing for reconnection with a missing part of the self" (p. 15). Shelley (1996) refers to *Frankenstein* as "my hideous progeny" (p. 173). Expressed this way, *Frankenstein* appears to be a loathsome self-aspect. Shelley may have regarded herself as a murderer and possibly held herself responsible not only for the death of her mother, but also for the deaths of her biological progeny. From this vantage point, *Frankenstein* can be interpreted as an orphan's story built upon the wish to literally re-create life from death. In marked contrast it can also be viewed as a desire to repeat death experiences. It can also be understood as a conflict in which aspects of life and death are both wished for and defended against. That is, Dr. Frankenstein's monster can be visualized as a split-off part of Shelley's self. If psychic conflicts are expressed in our dreams (Freud, 1900; Spotnitz & Meadow, 1976), then Mary's dream— that she claimed inspired her story—may provide information that may intimate answers and clarify these assertions.

the conflict in Mary's and Victor's dreams

In the dream that spawned Mary's narrative, the artist is "horror-stricken" when his creation shows signs of life:

> He would hope that left to itself, the slight spark of life which he had communicated would fade . . . into dead matter; and he might sleep in the belief that the silence of the grave would quench for ever the transient existence of the hideous corpse which he had looked upon as the cradle of life. (p. 172)

But in her story, Mary radically transforms Victor's behavior. Dr. Frankenstein flees in terror from the fiend he has created, believing his creation will destroy *him*. Mary changed Victor's actions from that of an aggressor who (in her dream) abandons the creature, leaving him for dead, to that of a victim who (in the story) is threatened by his creature. Mary's manipulation of Victor from killer to prey highlights a deep-seated ambivalence and doubt regarding Victor's/Mary's true self. This transformation suggests Mary's own uncertainty as to whether she was a victim or a murderer. It is certainly possible that she was both. Mary provided additional information about her own character when she decided, after 13 years, to share the earlier dream with her readers. During those 13 years, Mary's conflicts around loss, abandonment, and rejection had perhaps become more ambivalent and less certain. Mary may have been moving toward a more integrated psychic self since, through the years, death had been her constant companion. By the time of the 1831 printing of *Frankenstein*, which contained her dream, she was widowed and had only one surviving child. Perhaps, over time life and death made more sense to Mary and could co-exist more harmoniously within her psyche. The same was not true for Victor.

Shelley (1996) brilliantly captures the conflict between life and death as she describes Victor's determination to create life from death. Victor visits vaults and charnel houses in an effort to understand the human frame. Justifying his intrigue with decaying corpses, he says, "To examine the causes of life, we must first have recourse to death" (p. 30). Believing he is in search of the essence of life, he works in sheer isolation for nearly two years, unresponsive to contact from family and friends. Victor Frankenstein disconnects from life as he tries to infuse life into the creature he has assembled from death. "It was on a dreary night in November" that Victor finally saw the fruit of his obsession (p. 34). Quite remarkably, Victor was not elated but terrified and repulsed by the creature he had joyously created:

> I had desired it with an ardour that far exceeded moderation; but now that I had finished, the beauty of the dream vanished, and breathless horror and disgust filled my heart. Unable to endure the aspect of the being I had created, I rushed out of the room, and continued a long time traversing my bed-chamber, unable to compose my mind to sleep. (p. 34)

Victor could not understand this reaction to his creation and ran from the monster to escape into sleep. But the "wildest dreams" that disturbed his sleep may reveal the conflict of the story's author:

> I thought I saw Elizabeth [his beloved stepsister and future wife] in the bloom of health walking in the streets of Ingolstadt.

> Delighted and surprised I embraced her; but as I imprinted the first kiss on her lips, they became livid with the hue of death; her features appeared to change, and I thought that I held the corpse of my dead mother in my arms; a shroud enveloped her form, and I saw the grave worms crawling in the folds of the flannel. (p. 34)

Then Victor awakened and saw the monster staring at him:

> I started from my sleep in horror; a cold dew covered my forehead, my teeth chattered, and every limb became convulsed; when, by the dim and yellow light of the moon, as it forced its way through the window shutters, I beheld the wretch—the miserable monster whom I had created. He held up the curtain of the bed; and his eyes, if eyes they may be called, were fixed on me. (p. 40)

Victor is obsessed, not with life, but with death. Overcome by the site of the now living creature, he darted from it and dreamed of his dead mother. Collings (2000) contends that it was the maternal object that Victor was trying to create and the sight of it, in real time, destroyed his ability to remain sane. Victor bolted, abandoning the monster that, within the context of the story, posed no actual threat except that he wanted and needed Victor, as infants want and need their mothers. As Mary might have killed her mother in childbirth, Victor was not going to allow his hideous progeny to kill him.

Throughout the story, Victor's conceptualizations of life and death remain compartmentalized, i.e., split. Victor consciously sees himself as benevolent and the fiend as the destroyer. There is no fusion or compromise between the two; the creature is a split-off part of Victor. Mary's inclusion of her dream in the preface reveals that she, unlike Victor, has the potential for aggression on a psychic level. Her dream suggests that she could experience herself as a compilation of parts. It may have allowed her to integrate the murderous parts of her psyche with her creative energy and to see herself as separate from her dead mother, as Victor tragically failed to do. Mary's inclusion of her dream seems to have been healing and integrating in that it allowed her to acknowledge heinous, unwanted parts of herself.

idealization vs. integration

Victor had idealized the creature in fantasy. Upon seeing the creature come to life, Victor's zeal was instantly transformed into horror. Critics have suggested postpartum depression and the consequences of insufficient infant care for both mother and child as reasons for his distress (Moers, 1974). As in Mary's dream, a creature or infant who is abandoned will certainly wither and die. And a mother who has had insufficient mothering may also experience the birth and subsequent neediness of a child as a direct threat to her well-being. Mary Shelley watched several of her children perish. Although her own mother's death was an unconscious memory, Mary's lack of mothering was an ever-present reality. As a motherless child and a childless mother, one can conceptualize Mary as a living dead woman. She had never received and could not provide adequate nurturance. The prospect of giving what one has never known is experienced as an intense, narcissistic injury. Victor's horror at the site of his living, needy creature captures this dynamic as does his utilization of splitting to avoid unwanted feelings. For Victor, integration was out of the question because he was unable to remotely consider his destructive role in the monster's creation. Victor's internal world was perceived as shamelessly good, precisely because the destructive, hateful parts of him were projected onto the monster after the monster's creation. In fantasy, prior to his attaining life, the creature was presumably all good, i.e., idealized.

As Victor idealized his creature during its assembly, i.e., its creation, Mary too may have idealized her dead mother in fantasy. For both Victor and Mary, the idealization was a projection of a missing part of the self. This idea resonates with Klein's concept of the good and bad breast in which a young child, in fantasy, projects loving and persecutory fantasies upon the object in its infantile attempts to alleviate anxiety (Segal, 1988). Victor attributes to the creature that which he longs for—an idealized self in the form of an object. When the creature actually comes to life and is seen by Victor, his fantasy inevitably disintegrates. It is the *seeing*, the visualization of the fantasy, that is an annihilating moment for Victor. His creation of the monster forecloses the gap between the imaginary and the symbolic orders, and he strives to experience them simultaneously, which is impossible (Collings, 2000). Some fantasies cannot be realized without upsetting the natural order of life. At the very least, psychic disaster occurs, and at the very worst, physical ruin. As with incest, the desire for the oedipal parent creates irreversible destruction when it is actualized. Action is the only, truly threatening aspect of fantasy. By going into action, Victor, almost predictably, destroys himself with the creation of his idealized creature.

Idealization of the missing part of the self is at the crux of this heartbreaking story. Victor, an orphan like Shelley, tried to recreate the part of himself he had lost. Yet it is delusional to think that a beautiful creature could be designed from the scraps of rotting body parts, i.e., from death. It is, of course, Victor and Shelley's fantasy. Reality, in the form of the life-infused monster, not only shatters Victor's fantasy but brings with it severe retribution. According to Victor, his monster does not love him as he unconsciously anticipated. As the wretch is denied the unattainable love he seeks from his creator, he annihilates everyone to whom Victor freely gives love. The idealized individual becomes the persecutor when the fantasy, and the defense that supports it, disintegrates (Klein, 1986). The living monster is simultaneously a culmination of Victor's fantasy and the catalyst for its demise. Sadly, Victor's view of the world remains eternally polarized as he disavows his own involvement in the creature's atrocities.

Victor and the creature mirror each other in an intimate, yet destructive, recapitulation of the infantile fantasy of being fused with the early mother. This fusion results in mutual death. Victor eventually dies from a broken heart after suffering the loss of everyone he cherishes, and the fiend ultimately destroys himself subsequent to Victor's death. Yet the monster never physically threatens Victor directly; his persecution of Victor is indirect. Similarly, Mary was only circuitously responsible for the death of her mother. Other factors, including limited advances in obstetrics circa 1800, surely played a significant role in Wollstonecraft's death. In her psyche, however, Mary may have blamed herself for it. The deaths of Mary's three young children were also most likely caused, at least in part, by deficiencies in pediatric care and technology. Nonetheless, Mary's early experience of loss was engraved in her unconscious and played a significant role throughout her life. Ambivalence surrounded her role in her mother's death because she never really knew if she was the cause, i.e., the murderer or the consequence, i.e., an abandoned victim. Utilizing these deeply buried emotions, she created a story that universalized the fear of both abandonment and connection.

conclusion

A complex story of life and death, Shelley's *Frankenstein* captures man's yearning for a sense of self. In Shelley's view, a sense of oneness may be related to a belief that it is possible to connect with another. At the same time, connection is often accompanied by a potential for terror and annihilation. Hence connection, like separation, is both wished for and feared. Frankenstein's orphaned creature dies from unbearable isolation, dramatizing the depth of despair that can result from human loneliness arising from disconnection. *Frankenstein* is a story of longing. It is ultimately about the abhorrent realization that man is the master of his own destiny, yet slave to his unanalyzed repetitions. He faces his destiny and the consequences of his choices alone. The story of *Frankenstein* suggests that connection with another may exist only in fantasy. It is only through connection to all parts of oneself that individuals can ever hope to achieve significant integration and subsequent connections with others (Meadow, 2000).

references   Ainsworth, M. D. S. (1967), *Infancy in Uganda: Infant Care and the Growth of Love.* Baltimore: The Johns Hopkins University Press.

Almond, B. (1998), The monster within: Mary Shelley's *Frankenstein* and a patient's fears of childbirth and mothering. *International Journal of Psychoanalysis*, 79: 775–786.

Blum, H. (1979), The prototype of preoedipal reconstruction. *Freud and His Self-Analysis*. M. Kanzer & J. Glenn, eds. New York: Jason Aronson.

Bowlby, J. (1940), The influence of early environment in the development of neurosis and neurotic character. *International Journal of Psychoanalysis*, 7:154–178.

Brinich, P. M. (1993), Adoption from the inside out: a psychoanalytic perspective. *The Psychology of Adoption*. D. M. Brodzinsky & M. D. Schecter, eds. New York: Oxford University Press.

Brodzinsky, D. M. (1993), A stress and coping model of adoption adjustment. *The Psychology of Adoption*. D. M. Brodzinsky & M. D. Schecter, eds. New York: Oxford University Press.

Brodzinsky, D. M., D. E. Schechter, A. M. Braff, & L. M. Singer (1984), Psychological and academic adjustment in adopted children. *Journal of Consulting and Clinical Psychology*, 52(4):582–590.

Charon, S. R. (1994), Narratives told by adult adoptees regarding their experience of adoption. Doctoral diss., California School of Professional Psychology, Berkeley/ Alameda.

Collings, D. (2000), The monster and the maternal thing: Mary Shelley's critique of ideology. **Frankenstein:** *Mary Shelley*. 2nd ed. J. M. Smith, ed. Boston: Bedford/St. Martin's.

Fink, B. (1997), *A Clinical Introduction to Lacanian Psychoanalysis: Theory and Technique.* Cambridge: Harvard University Press.

Freud, A. & D. Burlingham (1944), *Infants Without Families.* New York: International Universities Press.

Freud, S. (1900), The interpretation of dreams. *Standard Edition.* London: Hogarth Press, 4 & 5.

Freud, S. (1907), Delusions and dreams in Jensen's *Gradiva. Standard Edition.* London: Hogarth Press, 9:1–96.

Gilbert, S. & S. Gubar (1979), *The Madwoman in the Attic.* New Haven: Yale University Press.

Hafetz, R. A. (2005), *Not Remembered, Never Forgotten: An Adoptee's Search for His Birthfamily: A True Story.* Baltimore: Gateway Press.

Hertz, J. E. (1996), In pursuit of authenticity—an adoptee's quest: a comparative study of the transference before and after reunion. Doctoral diss., Union Institute.

Hurst, W. (1999), A man of many losses: a study of fantasy, loss, and illusion. Final paper, Center for Modern Psychoanalytic Studies, New York.

Kirk, H. D. (1964), *Shared Fate.* New York: Free Press.

Klein, M., (1987), Notes on some schizoid mechanisms. *The Selected Melanie Klein.* J. Mitchell, ed. New York: Free Press.

Lacan, J. (1988), *The Ego in Freud's Theory and in the Technique of Psychoanalysis 1954–1955.* S. Tomaselli, trans. New York: Norton.

Levine, G. (1973), *Frankenstein* and the tradition of realism. *Novel: A Forum on Fiction,* 7:14–30.

Lifton, B. J. (1994), *Journey of the Adopted Self.* New York: Basic Books.

Margolis, D. (1996), *Freud and His Mother.* Northvale, NJ: Jason Aronson.

Meadow, P. W. (1984), The royal road to preverbal conflicts. *Modern Psychoanalysis,* 9:63–92.

Meadow, P. W. (1989), Object relations in a drive theory model. *Modern Psychoanalysis,* 14:57–74.

Meadow, P. W. (2000), Creating psychic change in analysis. *Modern Psychoanalysis,* 20:3–15.

Moers, E. (1974), Female gothic: the monster's mother. *Literary Women.* Garden City, NY: Doubleday.

Nobus, D. (2000), *Jacques Lacan and the Freudian Practice of Psychoanalysis.* London: Routledge.

Partridge, P. (1991), The particular challenges of being adopted. *Smith College Studies in Social Work,* 61:197–208.

Powell, K. & T. Afifi (2005), Uncertainty management and adoptees ambiguous loss of their birth parents. *Journal of Social and Personal Relationships,* 22: 129–151.

Priel, B., B. Kantor, & A. Besser (2000), Two maternal representations: a study of Israeli adopted children. *Psychoanalytic Psychology,* 17:128–145.

Quinodoz, D. (1996), An adopted analysand's transference of a 'hole-object'. *International Journal of Psychoanalysis,* 77:323–336.

Robertson, J. & J. Robertson (1989), *Separation and the Very Young.* London: Free Association Books.

Segal, H. (1988), The paranoid-schizoid position. *Introduction to the Work of Melanie Klein.* London: Karnac Books.

Shelley, M. (1996), *Frankenstein.* J. P. Hunter, ed. New York & London: Norton.

Silverstein, D. N. & S. Kaplan (1982), Lifelong Issues in Adoption. http://www.adopting.org/silveroze/html/lifelong_issues_in_adoption.html

Small, C. (1973), *Mary Shelley's* Frankenstein: *Tracing the Myth.* Pittsburgh: University of Pittsburgh Press.

Smith, J. M. (2000), Introduction: biographical and historical contests. Frankenstein: *Mary Shelley.* 2nd ed. J. M. Smith, ed. Boston: Bedford/St. Martin's.

Spotnitz, H. (1981), Aggression in the therapy of schizophrenia. *Modern Psychoanalysis,* 6:131–140.

Spotnitz, H. (1985), *Modern Psychoanalysis of the Schizophrenic Patient.* New York: YBK Publishers.

Spotnitz, H. & P. W. Meadow (1976), *Treatment of the Narcissistic Neuroses.* New York: Manhattan Center for Advanced Psychoanalytic Studies.

Steele, M., J. Hodges, J. Kaniuk, S. Hillman, & K. Henderson (2003), Attachment representations and adoption: associations between maternal states of mind and emotion narratives in previously maltreated children. *Journal of Child Psychotherapy,* 29:187-205.

Thomas, R. (1990), *Dreams of Authority.* Ithaca, NY: Cornell University Press.

van den Berg, S. (1997), Reading the Object: Freud's Dreams. PsyArt, http://www.clas.ufl.edu/ipsa/journal/1997_van_den_berg01.shtm.

Verrier, N. (1993), *The Primal Wound.* Baltimore: Gateway Press.

Verrier, N. (2003), *The Adopted Child Grows Up: Coming Home to Self.* Baltimore: Gateway Press.

Warshaw, S. C. (2006), Losing each other in the wake of loss: failed dialogues in the adoptive family. *Understanding Adoption: Clinical Work with Adults, Children, and Parents.* K. Hushion, S. B. Sherman, & D. Siskind, eds. New York: Jason Aronson.

Wieder, H. (1977), The family romance fantasies of adopted children. *Psychoanalytic Quarterly,* 46:185-200.

6735 Ridge Boulevard #6G
Brooklyn, NY 11220
barbdamato@aol.com

Book review

PSYCHOANALYTIC DISAGREEMENTS IN CONTEXT. Dale Boesky. Lanham, MD: Jason Aronson, 2008. 228 pp.

Psychoanalysis is beset with conflicts about differing theoretical and clinical approaches. Classical Freudians, Ferenczian relationists, Kohutian self-psychologists, intersubjectivists, Kleinians, Kernbergian object relationists, Sullivanian interpersonalists, and Spotnitizian modernists all passionately believe they have a theoretically and clinically superior therapeutic model. But does one model do a better job explaining the dynamic unconscious? Does one model offer a clinical approach superior to others? This question is especially important to analysts who believe that interpretation is central to cure because providing the correct interpretation—the most accurate explanation of the patient's unconscious—provides the basis for therapeutic change. In the past century psychoanalysts have invested enormous energy in disagreeing, and our literature is filled with arguments for the superiority of each model. But because there is no method for close comparison of different models at a clinical level, our debates are characterized by authors talking past each other, ultimately inhibiting our development of clinical theory. Drawing on the hermeneutic tradition, Dale Boesky articulates a method of *contextualization* to resolve some of these enduring polemical disputes.

In this book Boesky offers a methodology to examine the context out of which an analyst's inferential process emerges. Ideally, Boesky (2005) would like to "develop a consensually accepted canon of rules of evidence for deriving inferences from [a patient's] associations" (p. 835). How does the analyst make meaning out of what he observes, and how does he use that understanding to form interventions? "Context" is a meaningful coherence created through the connection, or weaving together, of bits of information. Context begins when

information is selected according to "contextualizing criteria,"
a collection of assumptions, theoretical convictions, or logi-
cal processes that guide the analyst's selection of data. Boesky
(2008) says, "By contextualizing criteria I mean all those inferential assumptions employed by the analyst" (p. 145). Contextualizing criteria are powerful though usually hidden from
view; often the analyst has no conscious awareness of these criteria during sessions, and rarely are these assumptions made
explicit during case presentations even though they form the
bedrock upon which psychoanalytic meaning rests. For Loewald (1971), for example, the belief that the unconscious
possesses a not-yet-understood internal coherence, or the as-
sumption that whatever transpires is personally motivated are
contextualizing criteria.

Looking at the logic of inquiry, Boesky cites Arlow's (1979)
suggestion that contiguity of data, repetition, multiple representations of the same theme, and a convergence of themes are
all contextualizing criteria used by analysts to form interpretations. "Context markers" are those informational attributes
that have previously proven useful. These markers, combined
with contextualizing criteria, become the basis for selecting
data for study. From an enormous pool of information the
patient presents, the analyst selects some bits for "foreground-
ing" while pushing the rest into the background. The patient,
arriving late or forgetting the check, a slip of the tongue, and
the first words spoken in the session are some familiar context
markers for analysts. Using this process of selective listening
(by the way, Boesky considers the description of the analyst's
listening innocent of memory, desire, or bias to be a fiction),
the analyst collects information and combines it to form "trial
contextualizations." At several points in a session the analyst applies these trial contextualizations to newly emerging
data to confirm a nascent conception of what's going on in
the patient's unconscious, or what's happening between the
patient and analyst in the session. "Contextual horizon" is a
term Boesky (2008) uses to describe "a group of associations
that are dynamically linked by the contextualizing criteria utilized by the analyst to capture the major dynamic urgency in
a given session" (p. 151). The visual metaphor of a horizon
describes both the linked information that together forms a

complete picture, while also describing the breadth and limits of the analyst's view. It declares what can be seen clearly along with an awareness of a blurry world of information we are unable to focus on, but which we know extends beyond our view.

Boesky suggests that our controversies flourish at a level of theoretical abstraction, but when we shift our attention to a close ("experience-near") analysis of a clinical case we have the best chance of understanding our theoretical and clinical differences. Boesky applies his contextualizing methodology to four case studies, and these chapters are certainly the most richly satisfying portion of his book. In a careful review of Patrick Casement's (1982) widely discussed paper on a patient's request for physical contact, he offers eight contextual criteria that are significant forms of missing evidence that together reshape our understanding of the case. In a thoughtful consideration of the work of the Boston Change Process Study Group (BCPSG) (1998), Boesky uses his close analysis of their methods of collecting and analyzing data to declare that their radically different epistemology—their belief in an indeterminate system of causality derived from non-linear dynamic systems (i.e., "chaos") theory—makes it impossible to meaningfully compare their results with a traditional conflict/defense model born out of a belief in psychic determinism. Because the two groups use totally different contextualizing criteria, Boesky calls such a comparison a "category error": it's comparing apples and oranges. Nonetheless, when examining a BCPSG case study, Boesky's reanalysis of their data within a traditional conflict/defense model appears to provide a superior explanation of patient/analyst interactions.

Boesky describes a case of his own involving enactment leading to his patient's recovery of an important memory. Boesky's seminal 1982 paper on acting out has long been a part of the modern psychoanalytic curriculum. He is one of a group of analysts who've spent years studying enactments—a group including Jacobs, Chused, McLaughlin, and Renik whom Chodorow (2004) describes as an emerging independent school of American intersubjective ego psychology. This group has integrated intrapsychic and interpersonal domains within a single theoretic model, an integrated model that appears completely consistent with

Spotnitz's conception of modern psychoanalysis. In Boesky's case presentation he uses his countertransference reaction to contextualize an emotionally charged transference-countertransference enactment. While his patient was reporting a dream Boesky dozes off, wakes up abruptly, and then disguises his having been asleep by asking the patient to clarify a point. Feeling deceptive, embarrassed, and humiliated over his professional lapse, over time Boesky says, he "gradually came to understand that the importance of my enactment was not only that I fell asleep but that I created a shameful secret of my own *for him to know about*" (p. 95, italics added). When the patient realizes Boesky's humiliation and shame at having lost control and fallen asleep—a shame similar to the patient's own losses of control—the patient reports a group of long-repressed painful memories of having wet and stained his pants as a small child. "It was as though he was saying that when he recovered his memory, he and I shared a shameful secret and we both wanted to cover up a stain. . . . Now it was I who was out of control and publically shamed" (p. 97). Considering this case from a modern psychoanalytic perspective, we would say the patient, by use of what Spotnitz calls the objective countertransference, induced in the analyst emotions concordant with his own. Feeling that he and the analyst were deeply similar and that the analyst rather than he had become the subject of humiliation, the patient lowered his defenses and "released" his dream from repression.

Having been deeply enriched by reading Boesky's book, I would like to share three personal observations. First, it seems that many psychoanalytic disagreements are fueled by emotions associated with identity and affiliation and reflect analysts' fundamental conservatism: when threatened by a competing theory, we often disagree passionately in order to strengthen and conserve our individual and collective (institutional) sense of identity. On those occasions we may not disagree primarily because we misunderstand the logic of the arguments at hand, but rather our disagreement facilitates our conservative, self-preservative impulses. One might wonder whether we, after having argued passionately for a century, really want answers to these polarizing questions. Boesky's book offers a refreshing alternative to these polemical disputes by providing a contextual basis for thoughtfully analyzing, clarifying, and sometimes resolving these disagreements. Nonetheless, to really employ Boesky's method to engage in comparative psychoanalysis requires a level of professional courage that can't be underestimated. In the face of these controversial conflicts, Boesky is to be commended for moving us toward a richer and more thoughtful analysis of our work.

My second observation is that analysts' contextualizing criteria, those bedrock assumptions that guide our selection of data, could be explicitly informed by decades' worth of psychoanalytic research. For example, the Boston Change Process Study Group (1998), while looking for the "something more" than interpretation affecting change in patients, developed contextualizing criteria based on patterns of interpersonal relatedness discovered through many decades of infant research. They might have been equally motivated to look for something more because a significant body of empirical research (e.g., Hoglend, 2004) demonstrates little association between interpretation and positive treatment outcome. If it isn't interpretation, what does cause the positive outcomes achieved by psychoanalysis? What is the "something more"? My point is that there is now a substantial amount of empirical research that can inform the analyst's contextualizing criteria, and it's important that analysts' personal and theoretical convictions be reshaped by this new knowledge. For psychoanalysis to consider itself a science, it needs to be able to alter its contextualizing assumptions based on the results of its own scientific inquiries.

My third observation is that the contextual horizon Boesky has charted might be profitably extended to more explicitly include the analyst's method for assessing therapeutic change in the patient. When employing Boesky's method of contextualization to compare two different clinical approaches to a patient, the question will likely arise: What if, after careful examination of their contextualizing methodology, two analysts offer different, but equally accurate, inferences about the patient's unconscious dynamics, and each analyst chooses a different intervention? How could we determine which therapeutic approach was better? Without a form of assessing change within the patient we'd never know. Spotnitz (1969) used the concept of progressive communication as an in-session measure of an intervention's effectiveness. If the intervention contributed to the patient's providing new material, gaining access to previously unconscious memories or feelings, this was regarded as a positive outcome. As analysts we could expand our criteria for assessing change in the patient within and across sessions, be explicit about how those assessments become context markers to guide technique, and use these assessments as evidence of therapeutic change.

Every psychoanalyst would profit from reading this book. Boesky's clear thinking is refreshing and his well-reasoned arguments are satisfying. This book can make an important contribution at an institutional level as well. Boesky (2002), whose Michigan institute began teaching a course on clinical evidence in 1988, suggests his contextualizing methodology become the basis for courses taught in comparative psychoanalysis. In addition, he recommends his contextualizing methodology be utilized within institutes to enhance thoughtful discussion of clinical cases and to clarify theoretical disagreements within the institute's preferred theory: "comparative analysis should begin with comparisons of disagreements between adherents of the same model instead of with disagreements of analysts of different models" (2008, p. 8). Just as tensions exist unnecessarily between psychoanalytic schools, similarly tensions arise within institutes where misunderstandings prevent profitable articulation and expansion of their particular psychoanalytic theory and clinical technique.

references   Arlow, J. (1979), The genesis of interpretation. *Journal of the American Psychoanalytic Association,* 27:193–206.

Boesky, D. (1982), Acting out: a reconsideration of the concept. *International Journal of Psychoanalysis,* 63:39–55.

Boesky, D. (1998), Clinical evidence and multiple models: new responsibilities. *Journal of the American Psychoanalytic Association,* 46:1013–1020.

Boesky, D. (2002), Why don't our institutes teach the methodology of clinical psychoanalytic evidence? *Psychoanalytic Quarterly,* 71:445–475.

Boesky, D. (2005), Psychoanalytic controversies contextualized. *Journal of the American Psychoanalytic Association,* 53:835–863.

Boesky, D. (2008), *Psychoanalytic Disagreements in Context.* Lanham, MD: Jason Aronson.

Boston Change Process Study Group (1998), Non-interpretive mechanisms in psychoanalytic therapy: the "something more" than interpretation. *International Journal of Psychoanalysis,* 79:903–921.

Casement, P. (1982), Some pressures on the analyst for physical contact during the re-living of an early trauma. *International Review of Psychoanalysis,* 9:279–286.

Chodorow, N. (2004), The American independent tradition: Loewald, Erikson, and the (possible) rise of intersubjective ego psychology. *Psychoanalytic Dialogues,* 14:207–232.

Hoglend, P. (2004), Analysis of transference in psychodynamic psychotherapy: a review of empirical research. *Canadian Journal of Psychoanalysis,* 12: 279–300.

Loewald, H. (1971), On motivation and instinct theory. *Papers on Psychoanalysis.* New Haven: Yale University Press.

Spotnitz, H. (1969), *Modern Psychoanalysis of the Schizophrenic Patient: Theory of the Technique.* New York: Grune & Stratton.

Dan Gilhooley

Books received

Blévis, Marcianne. *Jealousy: True Stories of Love's Favorite Decoy.* Olivia Heal, trans. New York: Other Press, 2008. 152 pp.

Clarke, Simon, Herbert Hahn, & Paul Hoggett, eds. *Object Relations and Social Relations: The Implications of the Relational Turn in Psychoanalysis.* London: Karnac, 2008. 210 pp. softcover

Frank, Claudia. *Melanie Klein in Berlin: Her First Psychoanalyses of Children.* Elizabeth Spillius, ed. Sophie Leighton & Sue Young, trans. New York: Routledge, 2009. 485 pp.

Joseph, Betty, ed. *Doubt, Conviction and the Analytic Process: Selected Papers of Michael Feldman.* New York: Routledge, 2009. 268 pp. softcover.

Obegi, Joseph H. & Ety Berant, eds. *Attachment Theory and Research in Clinical Work with Adults.* New York: Guilford Press, 2008. 529 pp.

Phillips, Adam & Barbara Taylor. *On Kindness.* New York: Farrar, Strauss & Giroux, 2009. 114 pp.

Piontelli, Alessandra. *Twins in the World: The Legends They Inspire and the Lives They Lead.* New York: Palgrave Macmillan, 2009. 253 pp. softcover.

Contributors

BERNSTEIN, JUNE, Ph.D., is director of public information at the Center for Modern Psychoanalytic Studies, dean of students at the Boston Graduate School of Psychoanalysis, and co-editor of this journal. She is a faculty member, training analyst, and supervisor at both institutes and practices in New York City and Boston. She has published numerous articles.

CHARLES, MARILYN, Ph.D., is a senior staff psychologist at the Austen Riggs Center and a psychoanalyst in private practice in Stockbridge and Richmond, MA. A poet and an artist, Dr. Charles has a special interest in the creative process and in factors facilitating creativity, and serves as co-chair of the Association for the Psychoanalysis of Culture and Society. She has presented and published her work widely and is the author *of Patterns: Building Blocks of Experience (2002), Learning From Experience: A Clinician's Guide (2004), and Constructing Realities: Transformations in Myth and Metaphor.*

D'AMATO, BARBARA, Psya.D., is a licensed psychoanalyst in private practice in New York City and in Brooklyn. She is a member of the faculty of the New York Graduate School of Psychoanalysis and the Center for Modern Psychoanalytic Studies, where she is a training analyst and supervisor.

DUNN, JONATHAN, Ph.D., is a licensed clinical psychologist and a member of faculty and training and supervising psychoanalyst at The San Francisco Center for Psychoanalysis. He is a co-chair of the center's admissions committee and teaches seminars on psychoanalytic technique, psychoanalytic process, validation, and beginning psychotherapy. He has been in private practice in San Francisco since 1986.

GREVEN, DAVID, Ph.D., is associate professor of English at Connecticut College. He is the author of *Manhood in Hollywood from Bush to Bush* (2009), *Gender and Sexuality in Star Trek* (2009), and *Men Beyond Desire: Manhood, Sex, and Violation in American Literature* (2005). His essays have appeared in such journals as *American Quarterly, Studies in American Fiction, Refractory, Genders, Poe Studies,* and *The Nathaniel Hawthorne Review.*

OPPENHEIM, JOSIE, M.A., NCPsyA, is a licensed psychoanalyst in private practice in New York City. She is a graduate of the Center for Modern Psychoanalytic Studies (CMPS), where she serves on its research committee, and is a founding member of the Adoption Circle at CMPS. She has taught writing and acting at Bank Street School for Children and The Stella Adler Studio of Acting and was cofounder and director of The Stella Adler Conservatory Theater. She is the author of numerous articles on child and adolescent substance use, early childhood education, and child development and has lectured in New York and Boston on adoption, the cultural context of dreams, and psychoanalysis and the creative process.